An Introduction to Grammar for Language Learners

Learning a foreign language is much easier when it is approached with a knowledge of language structure ("grammar"), but many students find grammar mystifying. This text explains points of grammar straightforwardly using examples from several widely studied languages, including English, so that students can see how the same principles work across different languages, and how the structures of different languages correspond both formally and functionally. The use of concrete examples makes grammar less abstract and easier to grasp, allowing students to relate what they are learning to knowledge that they already possess unconsciously; it simultaneously brings that knowledge up to a conscious level.

Don Ringe has been teaching undergraduate and postgraduate students for more than thirty years. In addition to historical linguistics and comparative Indo-European linguistics, he has taught a wide range of ancient and mediaeval languages. In 2012 he won the Ira Abrams Award for Distinguished Teaching at the University of Pennsylvania. He is the author or co-author of half a dozen linguistics books.

An Introduction to Grammar for Language Learners

DON RINGE

University of Pennsylvania

CAMBRIDGE
UNIVERSITY PRESS

CAMBRIDGE
UNIVERSITY PRESS

University Printing House, Cambridge CB2 8BS, United Kingdom

One Liberty Plaza, 20th Floor, New York, NY 10006, USA

477 Williamstown Road, Port Melbourne, VIC 3207, Australia

314–321, 3rd Floor, Plot 3, Splendor Forum, Jasola District Centre, New Delhi – 110025, India

79 Anson Road, #06–04/06, Singapore 079906

Cambridge University Press is part of the University of Cambridge.

It furthers the University's mission by disseminating knowledge in the pursuit of education, learning, and research at the highest international levels of excellence.

www.cambridge.org
Information on this title: www.cambridge.org/9781108425155
DOI: 10.1017/9781108605533

First published 2018

Printed in the United Kingdom by TJ International Ltd. Padstow Cornwall, 2018

A catalogue record for this publication is available from the British Library.

ISBN 978-1-108-42515-5 Hardback
ISBN 978-1-108-44123-0 Paperback

for Joy Famularo

Contents

Acknowledgments

I am grateful to Joseph F. Eska, Philomen Probert, Michael Weiss, and two anonymous readers for helpful comments on early drafts of this book; to Aaron Rubin for detailed comments on the Hebrew examples, which saved me from many errors; to Shizhe Huang and Anne Martin Montgomery for advice on and correction of the Mandarin examples; to Shizhe Huang for help with the excursus in Lesson 12; to Beth Randall, Ruth Randall, Joe Eska, and Chris Jackson for detailed comments on a late draft; and to two of the original readers for helpful comments on the penultimate draft. All remaining errors and infelicities are of course my own.

I have dedicated this book to Joy Famularo, the high school English teacher who taught me how to write a coherent essay. It seems only fair to acknowledge that I owe a good deal of my academic success to her. Of course she should not be held responsible for any flaws in this book (or in anything else I've written); on the contrary, if it weren't for Mrs. Famularo, you probably wouldn't be able to read this at all.

How to Use This Book

This is an introduction to the universal principles of grammar, illustrated with examples from a variety of languages. It can be used in several different ways, depending on circumstances.

The book is organized as a textbook for a course in grammar, and it can be used that way. An undergraduate class can cover the book in a semester of twelve weeks or so; a class of secondary school students might require more time. But in either case the instructor MUST be thoroughly familiar with the material. It is not necessary to have some command of all the languages used here to exemplify the principles. However, the instructor needs to be thoroughly familiar with the principles of grammar and with their application in detail in English and at least one other language (not necessarily one of those used for examples in this book).

In addition, the instructor will find it necessary to provide further examples and construct further exercises. If the students are all preparing to study the same language, the additional material should illustrate the structure of that language, whether or not it is one of those employed here. The instructor might also wish, or even find it necessary, to explore some of the topics introduced in this book in greater detail.

Alternatively, this book can be used as a framework to construct a course in the grammar of a particular target language. The first twelve lessons introduce basic concepts that are expressed (one way or another) in every language and should be covered no matter what the target language is; Lesson 14, on the English verb, should also be covered as background for discussing the verb system of the target language. The other lessons have been constructed so that they can be used individually, depending on how relevant to the target language they are.[1] If the target language belongs to the Indo-European or the Semitic family, or if it is an east Asian or west African language with little or no

---

[1] I am grateful to Joe Eska for suggesting that the book be modularized.

inflection (like Mandarin), such an adaptation will be comparatively easy. If the language belongs to some other family or is typologically very different, more work will be involved, but I hope that the inclusion of Navajo will at least point the way toward what needs to be done. For many languages much more attention will need to be paid to inflection. I have deliberately introduced the inflectional systems of my sample languages only in a piecemeal fashion, because the details of inflection are always idiosyncratic, and too much detail would make this entry-level book too hard to use. If a single language is being targeted, that consideration does not apply, at least not to the same degree.

Finally, readers can use this book for self-study, either by itself or together with a grammar of a target language. The advantage is that one can proceed at one's own pace; the disadvantage is that one has to figure things out for oneself and provide one's own supplementary examples. Motivation will of course be crucial.

1 | Introduction

What This Book Tries to Teach You

In the USA, and (I'm told) in some other English-speaking countries, grammar is no longer taught in schools; even classes in modern foreign languages sometimes try to teach with as little reference to formal grammar as possible. That is unfortunate for the following reason.

When you first start learning a new language, the number of new words you have to memorize in a hurry seems overwhelming; but actually the vocabulary is not the hardest part of a language to learn. True, most people need many dozen repetitions (in context) before they begin to recognize a foreign word automatically, but mere repetition will do the trick: if you put in the time and concentrate on what you're doing, you'll learn the words eventually.

However, it's much more difficult to learn the *structure* of a language – that is, its grammar – just by listening to it for hours. It wasn't always so. Up until the time you were about 7 years old, you really could learn a new language's grammar just by listening to it. Learning a language that way is called *native language acquisition*; any language acquired that way is a *native language*.

You have at least one native language; many millions of people have two or three, and at least a few million have four or more (although few of those people live in the USA or in other English-speaking countries). If a language is native to you, you have a *perfect*, but *unconscious*, knowledge of its structure, and you can use it automatically without any conscious control.

Unfortunately, languages can be learned natively only in childhood; for reasons that we still don't understand, it becomes harder and harder to learn a new language that way late in childhood, and at puberty the "window" for native language acquisition closes for good. So what do you do if you need or want to learn a new language after that? Some educational systems simply keep plugging away with direct exposure, figuring that that's the best you can do. For a few students – gifted language learners, especially those that already know two or three languages – that works well, but for most students it takes a long time and still yields only modest results.

Fortunately you can improve on the "direct method" by *combining* it with a knowledge of how languages *in general* are structured; if you can get explicit instruction in the grammar of the language you're learning, the results are better still. In effect, since you no longer have a subconscious ability to learn language structure natively, you're substituting a conscious knowledge of language structure in general, or of the structure of your target language in particular.

In Europe they know that and act on it; that is one reason so many Europeans speak multiple languages (typically including English) fluently. Classicists, too, understand the necessity of explicitly teaching grammar. Professional linguists use the same techniques to learn new languages rapidly. Those three communities are proof that combining the teaching of formal grammar with extensive practice really works. The hours of direct exposure are still necessary, of course; advocates of the direct method are not wrong about that. The trick is to approach all that practice with as much advance information about the structure as possible, so that you can understand what you're hearing in the shortest possible time.

This book is intended to provide basic information about language structure so as to make your task in learning a foreign language easier. I haven't told you everything that's known about any topic – not even everything that I know. The aim is to get just the basics into your head. I have deliberately avoided introducing any specific modern linguistic theory; this book is "pretheoretical" (unlike, for example, Soames and Perlmutter 1979 or Gelderen 2002). That is not because I have any doubts about the advantages of modern linguistic theory;

after all, real progress in the study of syntax began with Chomsky, and we have learned an enormous amount from generative and post-generative work in linguistics. But a pretheoretical approach is simpler, and I have tried to keep this simple. I have also kept the discussion as brief as I could, since too much verbiage is bound to bore people. An unfortunate result of that strategy is that the book can't just be read cover to cover, because most people can't assimilate the material that fast. There are exercises at the end of many lessons to help you work into the material, but you (or your instructor) should also spend time trying to find further examples in a language (or languages) of interest to you; that will make the grammatical concepts easier to remember and use.

You should try to internalize the important points listed at the end of many of the lessons. Repetition helps much more than intensive cramming.

What This Book Expects from You

I assume that you really want to find out about natural human language structure so as to better understand the language you're learning and make it easier to learn. If that's true, you should be willing to learn a fair amount of unfamiliar but not-too-hard technical material, provided that I can explain it and present it to you at a reasonable pace. There really isn't any alternative; language structure is the way it is, and you have to take it on its own terms to understand it.

If you dread grammar the way some people dread math, or if your brain shuts down when it's presented with something in a foreign language, you need to force yourself to engage with the material; you'll soon find that it's more accessible and less intimidating than you had thought. Remember, millions of people have learned basic grammar.

If you're afraid of making mistakes, summon your courage and choke down the fear, because in language learning *making mistakes and having them corrected is the main way you learn.* Your instructor should understand that and should cut you lots of slack.

If you find grammar dry and boring, go back to direct exposure without explicit grammar – but it will take you longer to get where you want to go.

It's important to realize that the grammatical terms introduced (and there are a lot of them) are not jargon intended to exclude the uninitiated; they're tools for discussing the details of language structure. If we didn't use them, we'd have to describe a familiar concept every time we needed to refer to it, and technical discussion would become practically impossible. (The same is true in every technical discipline, above all in the "hard" sciences.) There is an extensive glossary at the end of the book; you should refer to it whenever you need to. But you should also try to remember the terms that keep appearing on a regular basis.

It's also important to realize that, with some basic knowledge of grammar, sharp powers of observation, and patience, it's possible to make sense of the structure of any language you encounter, no matter how unfamiliar it is. Moreover, looking at the grammars of several languages at once can actually be easier than tackling them one by one, because languages are enough alike that the structure of one will help illuminate the structure of another. Some of the exercises ask you to look at data from languages you have (probably) never seen before, which have not been discussed in the text, and answer questions about them. You will find that you can make sense of them, working with the English translations given and bearing in mind that you can usually cut a linguistic form up into its component parts.

If you can get interested in language structure, encountering new languages can be a great deal of intellectual fun.

Mastering the material in this book will require substantial effort, but in the long run it will pay off by making the task of learning a language easier.

The Structure of This Book

The universal concepts of language structure will be introduced in naturally connected groups. Each will be illustrated by examples from (up to) six languages: English, Spanish, Classical Latin, Biblical Hebrew,[1] Navajo, and Mandarin Chinese.[2] I will usually give the Mandarin examples both in pinyin and in (simplified) characters, for the benefit of readers who are used to characters; examples in

---

[1] I have occasionally used words from later stages of Hebrew when no word for a particular concept is attested in the Bible.

[2] There are several Chinese languages, all obviously related to but not mutually intelligible with one another. Mandarin is the majority language in China and the official language; it is usually what people mean when they say "Chinese."

languages other than English will sometimes be accompanied by notes or a word-for-word gloss in order to make their (relatively unfamiliar) structures clearer.

These languages were chosen because English, Spanish, and Mandarin are important world languages widely spoken in the USA and elsewhere; Latin and Biblical Hebrew are historically important in Western culture; and Navajo, which is among the Native American languages of the USA that are still viable, is superficially very different in structure from all the others examined here.

Together these languages give a fairly good picture of the range of possibilities in human language. Latin has a significant amount of INFLECTION; that is, its verbs, nouns, and adjectives appear in different forms depending on their relationships to other words in the sentence. Spanish is a direct descendant of Latin and therefore resembles it in many details, but it has simplified the inflectional system. English is distantly related to Latin and Spanish, so its grammatical categories are similar, but it has simplified the inherited inflectional system even more. The remaining languages are not demonstrably related to those three, nor to each other. Biblical Hebrew has an inflectional system roughly as complex as that of Latin but very different in detail; Navajo has a more complex inflectional system than either; Chinese languages have no inflection at all.

Of course, you might be studying some other language. Your instructor will be able to provide you with relevant examples from that language. You could read only the sections about English and your target language (if it is one of those employed here); after all, that's the material you'll need to remember. But if your main goal is to get a good idea of what language structure is like, then read about all the languages, even though you won't be able to remember everything.

In the first twelve lessons and in the fourteenth (on the English verb system), new terms will be in SMALL CAPITAL LETTERS. In subsequent lessons, not only new terms, but also those that have been introduced in lessons of less general interest (such as those on the verb systems of languages other than English) will be introduced in the same way. (In Lessons 27 and 28 most technical terms are not marked, since they occur only in those lessons.) Throughout the book, examples will be in *italics*; translations will be 'between single quotation marks'; and ungrammatical examples – sentences that you just can't say – will be preceded by an asterisk (*). When I give word-for-word translations into English (in order to make examples in other languages easier to understand), I will put the translations of inflectional markers in SMALL CAPS.

Practical Notes on Pronunciation (for the Interested and Curious)

The sounds of a language can be described adequately only by scientific phonetics and phonology, and we will take a brief look at that approach in Lesson 27. But in the meantime you might want at least a bit of information about how the example sentences in these lessons are pronounced. It's not strictly necessary, so you can skip this section if you like; you can always refer back to it if something puzzles you.

To begin with, you should be aware that English spells its vowels unlike any other language on the planet; the vowels themselves are not particularly strange, but the way they are spelled is bizarre. Therefore, if you pronounce written material in any other language the way you would in English, you are certain to be wrong. We need to start from a better reference point.

Spanish

Spanish provides a much better reference point. Like hundreds of other languages, Spanish has a simple system of five vowels: *i e a o u.* You can approximate their pronunciation in English by pronouncing *i* as "ee", *u* as "oo", and the others as "eh, ah, oh". A better approach would be to listen to a native speaker pronouncing them. Audio files can be found at www.phonetics.ucla .edu/course/chapter1/vowels.html; you will see a chart with all the vowel symbols that phoneticians use. Click on each of the symbols that spell the normal Spanish vowels and you will access an audio file with a pronunciation of that vowel (not necessarily from Spanish, but in any case from a language with very similar vowels). The vowels of the other languages in our sample will be described below by reference to the Spanish vowels.

Consonants are somewhat less of a problem: many symbols have *approximately* (though not always exactly) the same pronunciation in numerous languages. Here are some notes on the most important points of Spanish pronunciation for a speaker of English to bear in mind.

Spanish has two r-sounds. At the beginning of a word *r* is heavily trilled; that is, the passage of air through the mouth makes the front part of the tongue hit the top of the mouth just behind the teeth several times in rapid succession. The same trill is spelled *rr* between vowels. In most other positions a single *r* is just a light tap of the tongue-tip against the top of the mouth just behind the teeth. The two Spanish *r*'s need to be distinguished, because the difference between them can make a difference in meaning; *pero* 'but' is a different word from *perro* 'dog'. The Spanish consonant *ñ* is approximately like the *ny* in English *canyon*; in Spain *ll* is approximately like the *lli* in English *million*, but in the Americas *ll* is pronounced exactly like *y*. The consonant *s* is always voiceless,[3] as in English *hiss*; there is no consonant like English *z* in Spanish. In the Americas the Spanish consonant spelled *c* before *e* and *i*, but *z* in other positions, is pronounced exactly like *s*; in Spain it is pronounced like the *th* of English *thin*. The spelling of k-, g-, and h-sounds is more complicated:

approximate Engl. equivalent	before *e* and *i*	elsewhere
k	*qu*	*c*
g (as in *get*)	*gu*	*g*
h	*g*	*j*

The written letter *h* is not pronounced at all in Spanish; for instance, *hombre* 'man' is pronounced as if it were spelled "ombre".

Latin

The Latin vowel system is like that of Spanish, but with an additional complication: each of the five vowels occurs both long and short. Long vowels are written in textbooks with a mark ¯ over them. The long vowels take about twice as much time to say as the short ones, so that from an English point of view the long vowels sound drawled and the short vowels can sound clipped. For instance, the first vowel of *mālus* 'mast' is much longer than the first vowel of *malus* 'bad', although otherwise they sound very similar – and as this example shows, a difference in

---

[3] See Lesson 27 for a description of voicelessness.

vowel length often makes a difference in meaning. Latin also has diphthongs, in which you begin with one vowel and slide into another; the two common ones are *ae*, pronounced roughly like the diphthong in English *height* or *chai*, and *au*, pronounced like the diphthong in English *house.*

For Latin consonants only a few notes are necessary. As in Spanish, *s* is always voiceless. Latin *c* is always pronounced like English *k*; *g* is always "hard," as in *get*; *v* is pronounced like English *w*; *qu* is "k" + "w", as in English.

Navajo

The Navajo vowel system is similar to the Latin system, with two major differences: there are only four basic vowels (there is no *u*), and in addition to being either long or short, vowels can be nasalized or not. Nasalized vowels are like the French vowels written *an*, *in*, *on*; in Navajo they are written with a hook beneath them, and long vowels are written double. For instance, in *háádę́ę́'* 'from where?' both vowels are long, and the second vowel is nasalized. Navajo also has a system of tones, according to which the pitch of the speaker's voice rises and falls; each vowel is spoken on a (relatively) high or low pitch. High tone is marked with an accent; thus both syllables in the word just cited have high tone (i.e. high pitch relative to the syllables around them in an utterance).

Many Navajo consonants and combinations of consonant-letters express approximately (though often not exactly) the same sounds as in English. Navajo *zh* spells the middle consonant of English *vision* or *measure.* Navajo *ł* is a voiceless l-sound, rather like a whispered *l*, but noisier; such a sound does not occur in English, but it does in Welsh, where it is spelled *ll.* (To find it on the UCLA phonetics website, look for the phonetic symbol [ɬ].) There is also a consonant spelled *gh*, which is like English (hard) *g* except that the tongue never actually reaches the roof of the mouth; it is exactly like Spanish *g* between vowels, but whereas in Spanish that is simply a special pronunciation of *g*, in Navajo it is a separate consonant. The *glottal stop*, spelled with an apostrophe ('), is a full consonant in Navajo; it is made by closing off the throat for a split second and then releasing it, as in the middle of the American English interjection *uh-uh* (meaning 'no'). Finally, Navajo has *glottalized* or *ejective* consonants, spelled *t'*, *tł'*, *ts'*, *ch'*, *k'*; as you might expect, they are made by producing the consonant more or less simultaneously with a glottal stop.

Mandarin

Mandarin, like Spanish, makes no distinction between long and short vowels. It uses the same symbols as Spanish, plus *ü*, which is a high front round vowel like French *u* or German *ü*. But the pronunciation of Mandarin vowels shifts dramatically depending on what other sounds they are adjacent to. For instance, *e* represents the sound spelled "eh" in English when it immediately follows *i* or *y*, but in most other positions it sounds like English "uh"; *u* is usually pronounced as in Spanish (= English "oo"), but after certain consonants it is instead pronounced like *ü*; and so on. The details are too complex to go into in these notes. More importantly, Mandarin is a tone language, like Navajo; but Mandarin has four tones, distinguished by marks over the vowel when spelled in the Roman alphabet. Using the vowel *a* as an example, *ā* has a high tone; *á* has a rising tone, usually somewhat drawled; *ă* has a low tone that dips in the middle; and *à* has a sharply falling tone and usually sounds clipped. The tone of a syllable is an integral part of it: if you change the tone, you produce a different syllable with a different meaning. For instance, *chū* means 'to come/go out', *chú* 'to divide', *chŭ* 'to get along with (someone)', and *chù* 'to touch'.

The way some Mandarin consonants are spelled is very different from the English system. Mandarin *s*, *sh*, and *ch* are much like English; but *c* is "ts", *z* is (roughly) "dz", and *zh* is approximately like English "j". In addition, there are three consonants that have no English equivalents: *x* is like "sh" pronounced simultaneously with a "y" sound; in the same way, *q* is like "ch" pronounced simultaneously with "y", and (Mandarin) *j* is like (Mandarin) *zh* pronounced simultaneously with "y". Distinguishing *x*, *q*, *j* from *sh*, *ch*, *zh* respectively takes a good deal of practice; you should get a native speaker to help you if you can.

Biblical Hebrew

What the Biblical Hebrew vowels were like depends on what era you're talking about. The traditional system of transcription that I use attempts to recover the pronunciation of about the fifth century BCE; it is possible that the distinction between long and short vowels had been lost by then, but if so, the transcription simply reflects a somewhat earlier stage of the language. Most of the system resembles that of Latin, but in addition there is a vowel *ə*, called "schwa," which is the indistinct vowel heard in the first syllable of English *about*, the last syllable of *sofa*, or the middle syllable of *terrible* or the last two of *tenement*. (Any vowel symbol can be used to spell schwa in English!) The vowels written small above the line (ᵉ, ᵃ, ᵒ) are hypershort versions of the corresponding full vowels.

Hebrew *š* is very much like English "sh"; scholars now believe that *ś* (*śīn*) was actually pronounced like Navajo *ł* (see above), although it eventually became identical with *s* (*sāmek*). In fact there are many different ways to pronounce the system of Hebrew consonants; for instance, you can pronounce Biblical Hebrew like Modern Hebrew, and many people do (just as Italians pronounce Latin – the ancestor of their language – like Italian). As in other such cases, the ancient pronunciation was somewhat different; the following notes describe what scholars think it was like in the fifth century BCE. The consonants *b*, *d*, *g* (as in *get*), *k*, *p*, *t* were pronounced roughly as in English in many positions, but after vowels they were lenited ("softened"). The lenited pronunciations and the transcriptions used in this book are:

basic consonant	lenited consonant	rough English equivalent
b	*ḇ*	*v*
d	*ḏ*	*th* as in *either*
g	*ḡ*	(no equivalant; = Navajo *gh*)
k	*ḵ*	(no equivalent; = *ch* in German *Bach*)
p	*p̄*	*f*
t	*ṯ*	*th* as in *ether*

Like Navajo, Hebrew had a glottal stop, here transcribed '; and scholars believe that the consonants transcribed *ṭ*, *ṣ*, *q* (*ṭēṯ*, *ṣāḏē*, *qōp̄*) were glottalized, corresponding to Navajo *t'*, *ts'*, *k'*.[4] Finally, Hebrew had two pharyngeal consonants,

---

[4] It is not certain that *ṣ* was a glottalized affricate [ts'] rather than a glottalized fricative [s'] in the fifth century BCE, but it was certainly an affricate in the Middle Ages and is one in Modern Hebrew. I am grateful to Aaron Rubin for helpful discussion of this point.

pronounced by pulling the tongue back to narrow the air passage behind it: the voiceless (roughly, whispered) one is transcribed *ḥ* (*ḥēṭ*), the voiced one with a reversed apostrophe ʻ (*ʻayin*). They are extraordinarily difficult for a speaker of English to pronounce, but they are common in Arabic, which is fairly closely related to Hebrew. If you can't find a speaker of Arabic to help you, examples can be found by surfing the UCLA phonetics website (referenced above) under the symbols [ħ] and [ʕ].

One final peculiarity of Hebrew spelling should be noted here. Even in the fifth century BCE, not all the consonants that were written were pronounced; in particular *h* at the end of a word or before another consonant was usually silent, and the glottal stop ʼ was also very often silent in those positions. There were also some combinations in which *y* and *w* were silent. I have *not* transcribed the silent letters of Biblical Hebrew, with the result that my transcription of the language diverges somewhat from the usual spellings.

2 | Sentences, Clauses, and Their Verbs

The Basic Unit of Discourse: The Sentence

People use language for all sorts of purposes, but on the most basic level they use language to say things. That's so obvious it sounds stupid – almost a tautology – but something important follows from it. Everything said is a statement, or a question, or a command, or an attempt to get somebody's attention, or an expression of strong emotion. Utterances in the last two categories are often very short. Typical English examples might include:

Hey!
Mom?!
You over there – yeah, you!!
Ow! Dammit!

What we should call utterances like that isn't clear, but it isn't very important, because they don't have much structure. The longer categories – statements, questions, and commands – are clearly types of SENTENCE. Every language offers an unlimited number of examples, because you can make up new sentences without limit. English sentences that you have probably never heard before include:

> *Sadly, no one wants my sardine-flavored ice cream.*
> *Do mice outwit you on a regular basis?*
> *Put that river down right this instant!*

Most of this book is about the structure of sentences, called SYNTAX, because in every language the structure of sentences and their parts is rigidly governed by the rules of the language's grammar.

Larger units of language can be recognized; for instance, in a conversation the speakers usually alternate, and each speaker's turn is a unit. But such larger units are not subject to the same hard-and-fast grammatical rules as sentences and their parts, so they are beyond the scope of this book.

Complex Sentences and Clauses

The examples of sentences given above are SIMPLE SENTENCES: each one is a single statement, question, or command. Simple sentences can be combined into COMPLEX SENTENCES; each of the simple sentences inside a complex sentence is called a CLAUSE. (A simple sentence by itself is a single clause.) Here is an English example:

> *When we got to the end of the rainbow we discovered that there wasn't any*
> *pot of gold.*

Clearly there are two statements being made, each describing an event, namely

> *we got to the end of the rainbow*

and

> *we discovered that there wasn't any pot of gold.*

By introducing the first clause with *when*, the speaker is indicating that the event described in the second clause followed the event described in the first clause. But further analysis is possible: the second clause in the analysis above also contains another statement, namely

there wasn't any pot of gold.

So actually there are three clauses in this sentence; we can diagram its structure as

[*When we got to the end of the rainbow*] [*we discovered* [*that there wasn't any pot of gold.*]]

with two clauses side by side, so to speak, and a third clause embedded in the second one.

We'll say more about complex sentences and clauses later; for the moment the important point is that you can combine simple sentences into complex ones, and you can analyze a complex sentence into its component clauses.

The Core of a Clause: The Verb

In English, and in many other languages, every clause must contain a VERB. The verb is the word or phrase that says what is going on in the clause, typically either an action or a state. Here is a sentence in our six sample languages, describing something that happened in the past, with the verb underlined:

E   *The students read fifteen books.*
S   *Los estudiantes leyeron quince libros.*
L   *Discipulī quīndecim librōs lēgērunt.*
H   *Qārə'ū hattalmīdīm ḥᵃmiššā 'āśār səp̄ārīm.*
N   *'Ółta'í 'ashdla'áadah naaltsoos yiyííłta'.*
M[1]   *Xuésheng kàn le shíwǔ běn shū.* 学生看了十五本书.

---

[1] In the first word of this Mandarin sentence, the syllable -*sheng* has no tone; that is typical (but not universal) for the second members of Mandarin compound words. The particle *le*, also toneless, indicates that the action was completed, while *běn* is the "classifier" for books. When a noun occurs with a numeral, a classifier must be inserted between them, and different classifiers accompany different classes of nouns. See Lesson 12 for more information on classifier systems.

What's going on in these sentences is *reading:* people have read something, which is an action. Another sentence:

E   *My grandfather is buying a coat.*

S   *Mi abuelo compra un abrigo.*

L   *Avus meus togam emit.*

H   *Qōne²'aḇ 'āḇī śalmā.*

N   *Shihanáli 'éétsoh nayiiniih.*

M³   *Wǒ yéye mǎi yí jiàn dàyī.* 我爺爺买一件大衣.

What's going on is *buying:* somebody is buying something, another action.

In the second sentence I had to use *toga* in the Latin translation and *śalmā* 'cloak' in the Hebrew because neither the Romans nor the ancient Israelites wore anything closely resembling our coat; in the Navajo and Mandarin translations I had to specify 'father's father' because those languages make you choose which grandfather you are referring to – there are completely different words for 'father's father' and 'mother's father', but no cover term for 'grandfather' – and in Hebrew I actually had to say 'the father of my father'.[4] Those are good examples of how vocabulary reflects culture. Grammar, however, almost never reflects culture: all six languages use verbs in exactly the same way.

There is one obvious difference between these languages in the sentences just given, though. In English, Spanish, and Mandarin the verb appears in the middle of the clause, right after the subject (i.e. the thing that "does the verb"; for a definition see the following lesson). In Latin and Navajo, however, it appears at the end of the clause, while in Hebrew it appears at the beginning. Those are the DEFAULT positions for the verb in these languages: the place where you put the verb when there's no reason to put it anywhere else. Roughly 40 percent of the world's languages have a default word order like that of English, Spanish, and French (verb in the middle of the clause), and another 40 percent like that of

---

[2] This is actually a participle (see Lesson 17), but the verb *yiqne* would occupy the same position in the sentence, which would then mean 'My father's father buys / will buy a cloak.'

[3] Mandarin *jiàn* is the classifier for clothing.

[4] There is no word for 'grandfather' in the Hebrew Bible; male ancestors in the male line are all called 'father'.

Latin and Navajo (verb at the end); other languages that typically put the verb at the end of the clause include Turkish and Japanese. A further 10 percent put the verb first, like Hebrew, Irish, and Welsh; the rest have other patterns, some of them complex, like that of German.

Recall that Spanish is a direct descendant of Latin. Evidently the default word order changed in the development from Latin into Spanish. That's not important for this book, but it's worth remembering that the grammar of a language can change over time – especially if you want to read the older literature written in your own language. For instance, Shakespeare's grammar is somewhat different from ours mainly because he was writing 400 years ago, and English has changed noticeably in the past four centuries.

Exercise

Divide up the following English sentences into clauses and identify the verb in each. In some cases the verb may be a short phrase.

1 *They didn't finish it because there wasn't enough time.*
2 *Who caught the biggest fish?*
3 *Take out the garbage.*
4 *If you don't know the answer, leave it blank.*
5 *Finally I got up over the hill, and I saw the most amazingly beautiful landscape.*
6 *I can't decide whether I should take the day off.*
7 *How you do it makes all the difference.*
8 *The fact that we don't know the exact number isn't relevant.*

To Be Remembered from Lesson 2

1 Most utterances in any human language are sentences.

2 Every sentence can be analyzed into clauses, each of which is built around a verb that expresses whatever is going on in the clause.

3 Different languages have different default word orders for their clauses.

Further Reading

A brief general discussion of sentences and clauses can be found in Gelderen 2002: 119–25; Quirk et al. 1980: 34–44 offer somewhat more extensive discussion, which is relevant also to Lessons 6 through 8.

3 | Subjects

Most verbs have identifiable SUBJECTS. For any verb X, its subject is whatever Xes (or Xed, or will X) in its clause; you could say that the subject is what "does the verb." Let's return to the second example sentence in the last lesson:

E   *My grandfather is buying a coat.*
S   *Mi abuelo compra un abrigo.*
L   *Avus meus togam emit.*
H   *Qōne 'aḇ 'āḇī śalmā.*
N   *Shihanálí 'éétsoh nayiiniih.*
M   *Wǒ yéye mǎi yí jiàn dàyī.* 我爺爺买一件大衣.

As we saw, the verb is *is buying* (/ *compra* / *emit* / *qōne* / *nayiiniih* / *mǎi*). The subject is whatever does the buying, and in this case it's *my grandfather* and its translations, which are underlined in this repetition of the sentence. In five of our languages it's the first thing in the sentence; in Hebrew it's the first thing after the verb. That's not universal, but it is typical: most languages tend to put the subject first, or right after the verb if the verb is first.

Note the way subject is defined here. It is *not* defined by reference to any real-world or imaginary situation. That is because we encounter pairs of sentences like the following:

I own this house.

This house belongs to me.

These two sentences describe a state of affairs, and it is exactly the same state; if the first is true, so is the second, and vice versa. Yet their structures are obviously different, simply because different verbs have been chosen. In the first sentence the subject is *I*, because the subject is whatever Xes (for any verb X), the verb X in this case is *own*, and I am the one who owns (the house). In the second sentence the subject is *this house*, because the subject is whatever Xes, and in this case the verb X is *belong*. In other words, subjects are defined entirely in terms of the structure of the sentence, not in terms of how they correspond to the real world. That is how language structure works: it's more or less autonomous, and you have to define its parts by their relations to each other, not by their relations to the external world.

In many languages the subject does not have to be expressed. Suppose we take the first example sentence in the last lesson and replace the subject *the students* with *we:*

E   <u>*We*</u> *read fifteen books.*

S   *Leímos quince libros.*

L   *Quīndecim librōs lēgimus.*

H   *Qārānu ḫᵃmiššā ʿāśār səpārīm.*

N   *ʾAshdlaʾáadah naaltsoos yíilta'.*

M   <u>*Wǒmen*</u> *kàn le shíwǔ běn shū.* <u>我们</u>看了十五本书.

The subject is whoever read the books, and that's *we*, or in Mandarin *wǒmen*, underlined in this repetition. But in the other translations of this sentence there is no word that translates *we*. Why?

The usual explanation is that you can omit the subject because it's referenced on the verb. It certainly is in all four languages. You say *leímos* in Spanish, *lēgimus* in Latin, *qārānu* in Hebrew, or *yíilta'* in Navajo only if the subject is 'we'. If you compare these verb forms with the ones that were used when the subject was 'the students', you will see that they are different: with a plural noun subject like 'the students', the forms are *leyeron, lēgērunt, qārəʾū,* and *yiyíílta'* respectively. So it's reasonable to say that *leímos* in Spanish means 'we read' by itself, without any need of a separate word meaning 'we', and so also with the other corresponding forms. These languages have SUBJECT-VERB AGREEMENT: the verb has a range of forms that "agree" with different kinds of subject (see Lesson 5 for further discussion), and if your language has subject-verb agreement you can often omit the subject without creating any ambiguity. Languages that can do that are called NULL-SUBJECT LANGUAGES; Spanish, Latin, Hebrew, and Navajo, as different as they are, are all typical examples of null-subject languages.

In a null-subject language you *can* use subject pronouns; but since you don't need to, you use them only to contrast the subject with something else, or for emphasis. Thus in Spanish 'I have' is usually just *tengo*; *yo tengo* means '*I* have', with heavy emphasis on 'I'.

So far, so good. But it turns out that not all languages with subject-verb agreement are null-subject languages, and not all null-subject languages have subject-verb agreement. Both French and German have subject-verb agreement, yet you cannot omit the subject in a statement or question in either French or German. For instance:

F   *Nous avons lu quinze livres.*
G   *Wir haben fünfzehn Bücher gelesen.*

In French, verb forms ending in *-ons* always agree with the subject *nous* 'we', yet the subject cannot be omitted in statements or questions; neither can German subjects. Conversely, Mandarin has no subject-verb agreement (because Chinese languages have no inflection at all), yet you normally omit the subject whenever it can be inferred from the context! For instance:

Wǒ yéye zuótiān qù le chénglǐ.   Zài nàli mǎi le yí jiàn dàyī.
我爺爺昨天去了城里.   在那里买了一件大衣.

'My grandfather went to town yesterday. There he bought a coat.'

The verbs are underlined. The subject 'my grandfather', with dotted underlining, occurs only in the first sentence; in the second it is not even replaced by *tā* 'he' – no subject is expressed at all, because it can be supplied from the context. (*Zài nàli* literally means 'being there'.) Of course even English can do that if the two clauses are connected by *and*, e.g.:

She took the hammer and __ broke the glass.

in which *she* is the (unexpressed) subject of *broke*. (So also in German and French.) But if the clauses are not so closely joined, the subject must be repeated, e.g.:

She grabbed the hammer. For a moment she hesitated; then she broke the glass.

In a null-subject language like Mandarin only the first of those subjects must be expressed.

To sum up: it is very convenient for a language that has subject-verb agreement to have null subjects too, and many do, but not all. Conversely, there are other ways that a language can get away with null subjects, even if it is not quite as convenient. Here is a table of the languages discussed in this lesson, classifying them by whether they have subject-verb agreement and are null-subject languages:

		S-V agreement	
		Yes	No
Null subj.	Yes	Spanish, Latin, Hebrew, Navajo	Mandarin
	No	English, German, French	

Worldwide, null-subject languages greatly outnumber those that are not.

There are two other things about subjects that should be said here. In an English sentence like *it's raining*, the subject is *it*; but exactly what does *it* refer to? It doesn't really refer to anything; it's a DUMMY SUBJECT, and it's there only because in English you have to have a subject whether it means anything or not. From what's been said above, it won't surprise you to learn that German and French also require a dummy subject in this sentence (*es regnet* and *il pleut* respectively). It also won't surprise you that our other sample languages do not require a subject for this verb – in fact Spanish and Latin can't express one:

E   *It rained.*
S   *Llovió.*
L   *Pluit.*
N   *Nahóółtą́.*
M   *Xiàyǔ.* 下雨.

The sentence 'it rained' does not occur in the Hebrew Bible; in later Hebrew one says *yāraḏ gešem* 'rain fell'. In Navajo you can also say *tó nááłtą́* 'water fell', and in Mandarin you can also say *tiān xiàyǔ* 天下雨 'the sky rained'.

The other detail has to do with commands. In many (most?) languages the subject is usually dropped in commands, even if the language is not null-subject. All six of our languages do that:

E[1]   *Give me the book.*

S   *Dame el libro.*   (or, more politely, *Me dé el libro.*)

L   *Dā mihi librum.*

H   *Tēn lī 'eṯ-hassēp̄er.*   (*l-ī* 'to-me')

N   *Naaltsoos shaa ní'aah.*   (*sh-aa* 'me-to')

M   *Gěi wǒ shū.* 给我书.

The verbs are underlined; the subject is understood to be *you* (/ *tú* / *tū* / *'attā* / *ni* / *nǐ*), but it is not expressed. In the languages in which the verb usually follows the subject you can see from the word order that there is no subject, because the verb is first. But even in Latin, where the verb is usually found at the end of the clause, verbs tend to be placed at the beginning of commands.

Navajo, however, is a little different from the others. For one thing, the verb is still at the end of the sentence; but there is another difference as well. Spanish, Latin, and Hebrew commands are expressed with a special verb form called the IMPERATIVE; English commands are also different from statements because the basic form of the verb is used. Compare the following sentences, which are ordinary statements:

E   *You are giving me the book.*

S   *Me das el libro.*   (polite *Usted me da el libro.*)

L   *Mihi librum dās.*

H[2]   *'Attā nōṯēn lī 'eṯ-hassēp̄er.*

---

[1] In some colloquial varieties of American English, *give* is being replaced by *gift*, at least in some of its meanings. The new verb appears in the same grammatical constructions as the old one.

[2] This Hebrew sentence actually contains a participle; it literally says 'You (are) giving ...', with the verb 'be' suppressed. That is the usual way of expressing present time in Biblical Hebrew; see Lesson 17 for further discussion.

Navajo has no special imperative form; commands and statements are identical:

N   *Naaltsoos shaa ní'aah.*
'You are giving me the book.'

The real-world context disambiguates.

Exercise

Identify the subject in each of the following sentences. If the sentence has more than one clause, identify the subject of each clause.

1 *Why did you do such a thing?*
2 *The man in the yellow hat finally found George in the closet.*
3 *I don't think the law should allow that.*
4 *The weatherman said it's going to snow tomorrow.*
5 *That statement doesn't make any sense.*
6 *Please sit down and be quiet.*
7 *John and Mary have eloped.*
8 *Bert went to Chicago and found a better job.*

To Be Remembered from Lesson 3

1 For any verb X, the subject is whatever Xes (or Xed, or will X).
2 In many languages the form of the verb changes depending on what the subject is; that is called subject-verb agreement.
3 In many languages the subject does not need to be expressed if it can be understood from the form of the verb or from context; those are called null-subject languages.
4 You might expect that null-subject languages would have subject-verb agreement, while languages without subject-verb agreement could not omit the subject, but in fact there is no correlation between those two phenomena.

5 Languages that are not null-subject typically have meaningless ("dummy") subjects for weather verbs and other naturally subjectless verbs.

6 Even languages that are not null-subject often omit the subject in commands. Many languages have special verb forms, called imperatives, to express commands.

Further Reading

Butt and Benjamin 2011: 331–33 is a good discussion of when and when not to use subject pronouns in Spanish. Quirk et al. 1980: 951–61 discuss some other types of dummy subjects in English, some of them quite complex.

4 Noun Phrases; Number

The term "verb" actually has a double meaning. We've been using it to indicate a particular grammatical FUNCTION in a clause: we've identified it as the central word or short phrase that indicates what's going on in that clause. But words can also be considered in isolation from their clauses, and "verb" is also the name of the major class of words that typically perform the verb function in clauses. If you're talking about English, you can say, "*be, have, go,* and *discover* are verbs," and it will always be true because those words belong to the class of verbs in English.

The term "subject" isn't like that: it indicates *only* a function in a clause, namely whatever Xes, where X is the verb of the clause. It does not indicate a class of words or phrases independently. For instance, in the example sentences in the last two lessons *my grandfather* was a subject, but you can also use the same phrase in non-subject functions. For instance, it clearly isn't the subject in either of these sentences:

> *I love my grandfather.*   (subject is *I*)
> *Give my grandfather the book.*   (subject *you* is unexpressed)

So we need a term for phrases like *my grandfather* independently of whatever function they're performing in a clause.

Phrases that can be subjects (among other functions) are called NOUN PHRASES. A typical noun phrase is built around a NOUN; for instance, the noun phrase *my grandfather* is built around the noun *grandfather*. A noun prototypically refers to some real-world or imaginary entity or idea; typical English nouns include *cat, ghost, hatred* (an abstract entity, but all too real), *people, indecision*, and so on. A language with a small vocabulary, like Classical Latin, will have hundreds of verbs but thousands of nouns, simply because there are so many real-world entities that you need to refer to.

Noun phrases can be long and complex. For instance, *the man in the yellow hat*, which appeared in the exercises to the last lesson, is a noun phrase (built around the noun *man*, and the subject of its verb in the exercise). You can even embed whole clauses inside a noun phrase; an English example is *the book which I haven't read yet* (built around the noun *book*; the subject of the embedded clause is *I*). On the other hand, a noun phrase can be just a noun. Names, such as *John* and *Oklahoma*, are nouns that are usually used as noun phrases by themselves; some other nouns, like *people*, often occur as whole noun phrases. So far as I know, these statements are true of all languages. We can investigate the internal structure of noun phrases later; for now we just need to be able to identify them.

English, Spanish, Latin, and Hebrew mark NUMBER on nouns, distinguishing SINGULAR (indicating one) from PLURAL (indicating more than one). Here are some typical examples of nouns with their plurals:

English	Spanish	Latin[1]	Hebrew
daughter, daughters	*hija, hijas*	*fīlia, fīliae*	*baṯ, bānōṯ*
book, books	*libro, libros*	*liber, librī*	*sēp̄er, səp̄ārīm*
hand, hands	*mano, manos*	*manus, manūs*	*yāḏ, yāḏayim*
dog, dogs	*perro, perros*	*canis, canēs*	*keleḇ, kəlāḇīm*
law, laws	*ley, leyes*	*lēx, lēgēs*	*tōrā, tōrōṯ*
wolf, wolves	*lobo, lobos*	*lupus, lupī*	*zə'ēḇ, zə'ēḇīm*
sheep, sheep	*oveja, ovejas*	*ovis, ovēs*	*'ayil, 'ēlīm*

---

[1] I here give the Latin NOMINATIVE forms, used when the noun is the subject of a verb; other forms will be mentioned and discussed in Lesson 6 and later lessons.

ox, oxen	buey, bueyes	bōs, bovēs	par, pārīm
foot, feet	pie, pies	pēs, pedēs	regel, raglayim
woman, women	mujer, mujeres	mulier, mulierēs	'iššā, nāšīm

The Spanish system is simple and consistent: the plural adds *-s*, unless the noun ends in a consonant, in which case *-es* is added. English is only a little more complicated. The vast majority of noun plurals have an ending spelled *-(e)s*; its pronunciation varies but is usually predictable from the last sound of the noun, so those noun plurals are just as straightforward as the Spanish ones. However, a handful of nouns with plurals in *-(e)s* change their shape as well as adding the ending; for instance, about twenty nouns ending in *-f* change that consonant to *-v-* in the plural, like *wolf* and *knife*. Another handful of nouns, mostly denoting animals, have no marker in the plural, like *sheep* and *deer*. In addition, seven nouns – *man*, *woman*, *mouse*, *louse*, *goose*, *tooth*, and *foot* – construct the plural by changing their vowels, and the nouns *ox* and *child* have unique plurals. But the plural means exactly the same thing no matter how it is formed; *hands* and *feet*, for instance, are used in all and only the same ways grammatically. In effect, English nouns are sorted into arbitrary classes, called LEXICAL CLASSES, on the basis of how they construct their plurals. However, one of those classes is the default class: not only does it include the vast majority of nouns, a noun belongs to it automatically unless specified otherwise.

Latin nouns are also divided into lexical classes, but in Latin there is no default class: you simply learn a noun's lexical class when you learn the noun. Moreover, whereas English nouns are endingless in the singular, you can see from the table above that Latin nouns very often have endings both in the singular and in the plural, so that instead of adding an ending in the plural you replace one ending with another. The Hebrew system is intermediate in complexity, and it introduces another wrinkle. Like many European languages, Hebrew assigns every noun to one of two GENDERS, masculine and feminine, partly on the basis of biological sex – nouns denoting females are normally feminine – and partly arbitrarily.[2] A large number of feminine nouns end in *-ā*,

---

[2] The same is true of Spanish and Latin, and Latin has a third gender, neuter; but gender assignment has no impact on the formation of Spanish plurals, while in Latin the relationship between genders and lexical classes is complex. See further Lesson 12.

and most of those nouns construct their plurals by replacing -*ā* with -*ōṯ*. Most other nouns construct their plurals by adding -*īm*. But there are a great many individual irregularities, so that the system is simple in principle but complex and quirky in detail.

Navajo does not indicate pluralization on nouns, and Mandarin usually does not; thus Navajo *naaltsoos* and Mandarin *shū* 书 can mean 'book' or 'books', Navajo *łééchąą'í* and Mandarin *gǒu* 狗 can mean 'dog' or 'dogs', and so on. The Mandarin pluralizer -*men* 们 can be used with nouns indicating human beings, but its use is very restricted and specialized; see Yip and Rimmington 1997: 10 for discussion.

There are languages that have not only plural forms of nouns, but also DUALS, indicating two, or (in some languages) a structured pair. In fact the Hebrew plurals in -*ayim* given in the table above were originally duals; that is why they appear on nouns meaning 'hand' and 'foot'. In Biblical Hebrew the distinction between dual and plural has largely broken down for nouns denoting paired body parts (though *yōmayim* 'two days' is still distinguished from *yāmīm* 'days', and a few other nouns still make that distinction), but there are languages that mark dual number on nouns consistently, including Ancient Greek, Sanskrit, and Eskimo-Aleut languages. A very few languages have more complex number systems.

Exercise

Here are some nouns and their plurals from an unfamiliar language. How does that language mark number on nouns? Does the distribution of singular and plural markers have any relationship to the meanings of the nouns? If so, describe the relationship.

	singular	plural
'child'	*mtoto*	*watoto*
'wife'	*mke*	*wake*
'stranger'	*mgeni*	*wageni*
'widow'	*mjane*	*wajane*

	singular	plural
'sick person'	mgonjwa	wagonjwa
'old man'	mzee	wazee
'cook'	mpishi	wapishi
'European'	Mzungu	Wazungu
'human being'	mtu	watu
'tree'	mti	miti
'date palm'	mtende	mitende
'banana plant'	mgomba	migomba
'mountain'	mlima	milima
'door'	mlango	milango
'town'	mji	miji
'foot'	mguu	miguu
'bird'	ndege	ndege
'banana'	ndizi	ndizi
'drum'	ngoma	ngoma
'strength'	nguvu	nguvu
'road'	njia	njia
'house'	nyumba	nyumba
'knife'	kisu	visu
'book'	kitabu	vitabu
'finger'	kidole	vidole
'bed'	kitanda	vitanda
'hut'	kibanda	vibanda
'island'	kisiwa	visiwa
'thing'	kitu	vitu
'egg'	yai	mayai
'flower'	ua	maua
'knee'	goti	magoti
'field'	shamba	mashamba
'answer'	jibu	majibu
'grass'	—	majani
'water'	—	maji
'milk'	—	maziwa

	singular	plural
'oil'	–	*mafuta*
'disease'	*ugonjwa*	*magonjwa*
'size'	*ukubwa*	–
'beauty'	*uzuri*	–
'badness'	*ubaya*	–
'old age'	*uzee*	–
'flour'	*unga*	–
'porridge'	*ugali*	–
'soil'	*udongo*	–

To Be Remembered from Lesson 4

1 Noun phrases are phrases that can be subjects of verbs.
2 Typical noun phrases include a noun; they can also include further items that modify or specify further the meaning of the noun.
3 Some languages mark pluralization on nouns; others do not. A fairly small minority of languages also mark dual number.

Further Reading

Quirk et al. 1980: 165–87 describe English noun plurals in detail; Corbett 2000 is a good worldwide survey of grammatical number.

5 | Pronouns and Subject-Verb Agreement

There is one special category of noun phrases that is very important. When the same entity keeps coming up in a discourse, we don't usually repeat the noun phrase that refers to it; instead we substitute a PRONOUN. For instance, in English we don't say

John said John didn't care, but I don't think John meant it.

I don't think you even *can* say that, if all the *John*s refer to the same person. (That's why I put an asterisk at the beginning.) Instead, we substitute *he* for *John* after the first instance:

John said he didn't care, but I don't think he meant it.

Pronouns that substitute for other noun phrases like that are called THIRD-PERSON pronouns (e.g. English *he, she, it, they*). There are also pronouns for the SECOND PERSON (in English, *you*), which is the person or people the speaker is talking to, and for the FIRST PERSON (*I* and *we*), which is the speaker or a group that includes the speaker. Once again these statements are true of all the languages that I've encountered; this is part of the basic structure of a natural human language.

Most languages mark number on pronouns, even if they do not do so on nouns; for instance, both Navajo and Mandarin indicate pluralization of pronouns. In many languages plural marking of pronouns is not straightforward. For instance, in English *we* is the plural corresponding to *I*, and *they* is the plural corresponding to *he*, *she*, and *it*, but there is no obvious separable piece that means 'plural', like the noun ending *-(e)s*; a form like *we* is an indivisible unit that indicates 1st person and plural simultaneously.

Here is a chart of the 1st-, 2nd-, and 3rd-person pronouns of our six sample languages.

	English	Spanish	Latin
1st singular	*I, me*	*yo, me, mí*	*ego, mē*, etc.
1st plural	*we, us*	*nosotros (-as), nos*	*nōs*, etc.
1st & 2nd	[use 1st pl.]	[use 1st pl.]	[use 1st pl.]
2nd singular	*you*	*tú, te, tí; usted, lo, la, le*	*tū, tē*, etc.
2nd plural	*you*	*vosotros (-as), os;* *ustedes, los, las, les*	*vōs*, etc.
3rd singular	*he, she, it; him, her*	*él, ella; lo, la, le*	*is, ea, id*, etc.
3rd plural	*they, them*	*ellos, ellas; los, las, les*	*eī, eae, ea*, etc.

	Hebrew	Navajo	Mandarin	
1st singular	*'ānōḵī, 'ᵃnī*[1]	*shí*	*wǒ*	我
1st plural	*'ᵃnaḥnū*	*(da)nihí*	*wǒmen*	我们
1st & 2nd	[use 1st pl.]	[use 1st pl.]	*zánmen*	咱们
2nd singular	*'attā, 'att*	*ni*	*nǐ; nín*	你；您
2nd plural	*'attem, 'atten*	*(da)nihí*	*nǐmen*	你们
3rd singular	*hū, hī*	*bí, hó*	*tā*	他[2]
3rd plural	*hēmmā, hēnnā*	*(daa)bí, (daa)hó*	*tāmen*	他们

As you can see, the systems are very different from one another. The Mandarin system is the simplest: 1st person is indicated by *wǒ*, 2nd person by *nǐ*, and 3rd person by *tā*; plurality is indicated by *-men*. There are only two

---

[1] There seems to be no functional difference between these two forms.

[2] This syllable is actually written with different characters depending on whether it refers to a male or female person or to an object (and sometimes further distinctions are made). However, that is a peculiarity only of the writing system; it is not linguistically real. You need to remember that language is primarily spoken; writing is only a way of *representing* language, and writing systems vary in how well they do that and in where they fall short. See also footnote 7 below and Lesson 29 at the end of this book.

complications: there is a special 2nd-person polite form *nín* (only in the singular), and some speakers have a special plural form *zánmen* for 'we' when the person being spoken to is included in 'we'. That is called an INCLUSIVE 1st-person plural (naturally enough); speakers of those dialects use *wŏmen* only when the person being spoken to is not included, so for them it is an EXCLUSIVE 1st-person plural. Some other languages make that distinction; many do not.

The Navajo system is also simple but is differently constructed. Surprisingly, there is only a single form for plural 1st and 2nd persons;[3] that is less ambiguous than you might expect, because 1pl. and 2pl. subjects are marked differently on the verb, so that the most important distinction – who is doing what – is clear. The usual 3rd-person form, both singular and plural, is *bí* 'he/she/it/they'; *hó* 'he/she' is only used to refer to animate referents, usually people, and is useful for distinguishing two 3rd persons in the same discourse. The prefix *da(a)-* is DISTRIBUTIVE in meaning; it can be translated roughly as 'each' in English.

The Hebrew system introduces the complication of gender: all the 2nd- and 3rd-person pronouns have two forms, one for masculine gender and one for feminine. Feminine forms are used to address and refer to female persons; in addition, 3rd-person feminine forms are used when referring to a noun phrase that is built around a noun assigned to the feminine gender (see Lesson 4).

The other sample languages typically have multiple forms for each person-and-number combination. We'll discuss them in more detail in the following lessons, but two of the Spanish distinctions can be noted here. Like Mandarin, Spanish has special polite forms for the 2nd person; in the chart they are separated from the "familiar" forms by a semicolon. In Spanish they are used far more often than in Mandarin; you wouldn't necessarily use Mandarin *nín* speaking to someone you don't know unless the person were obviously elderly, but in Spanish you use *usted* and *ustedes* with everyone you're not on familiar terms with (except small children). That's really a cultural distinction, not a structural one. Like Hebrew, Spanish also has different masculine and feminine forms for various pronouns. (Latin makes gender distinctions in pronouns only in the 3rd person, like English.)

---

[3] The same peculiarity recurs in many other Athabaskan languages, the family to which Navajo belongs (though not in all); it was clearly inherited from their common ancestor without change, so the system can't be critically dysfunctional.

Finally, the pronoun system plays a major part in subject-verb agreement (see Lesson 3). In Spanish, Latin, Hebrew, and Navajo the verb agrees in person and number with its subject. Here is the full list of Spanish and Latin forms of the present tense of 'read', given in the traditional order:

		Spanish		Latin
1sg.	(*yo*) *leo*	'I read / am reading'	(*ego*) *legō*
2sg.	(*tú*) *lees*	'you (sg.) read', etc.	(*tū*) *legis*
3sg.	(*él / ella / mi abuelo / usted*, etc.) *lee*	(*is / ea / avus meus*, etc.) *legit*
1pl.	(*nosotros*) *leemos*	(*nōs*) *legimus*
2pl.	(*vosotros*) *leéis*	(*vōs*) *legitis*
3pl.	(*ellos / ellas / ustedes*, etc.) *leen*	(*eī / eae / avī*, etc.) *legunt*

This is a partial PARADIGM of the verb 'read' in those languages; a full paradigm would include all forms of the verb.

An unusual feature of Spanish is that the polite 2nd-person forms trigger 3rd-person agreement on the verb. That is because *usted* 'you [sg. polite]' was originally an ALLEGRO (i.e. rapid-speech) form of *vuestra merced* 'your grace', the phrase used to address noblemen. This is a good example of how historical accidents can leave traces in a language's grammar.

Note that the "etc." in the list of 3rd-person subjects (both singular and plural) is important: *any* subject that is neither 1st nor 2nd person is 3rd person. In other words, the 3rd person is the default person in any language's grammar.

Hebrew distinguishes masculine and feminine forms of verbs except in the 1st person. The Hebrew agreement markers are partly PREFIXES (attached before the lexical part of the verb form) and partly SUFFIXES (attached after it).

1sg.	(*'ānōk̲ī*)[4] *'eqrā* 'I read'	1pl.	(*"naḥnū*) *niqrā*
2sg. m.	(*'attā*) *tiqrā* 'you (masc. sg.) read'	2pl. m.	(*'attem*) *tiqrə'ū*
2sg. f.	(*'att*) *tiqrə'ī* etc.	2pl. f.	(*'atten*) *tiqrenā*
3sg. m.	(*hū*, etc.) *yiqrā*	3pl. m.	(*hēmmā*, etc.) *yiqrə'ū*
3sg. f.	(*hī*, etc.) *tiqrā*	3pl. f.	(*hēnnā*, etc.) *tiqrenā*

---

[4] Although a Hebrew verb is usually first in its clause and is followed by an unemphatic subject (see Lessons 2 and 3), a heavily emphasized word is often put before the verb. Since the pronouns are used only for heavy emphasis, they normally appear first on the rare occasions when they appear at all.

Navajo has a single form for all 3rd-person subjects, whether singular or plural. In Navajo the lexical part of the verb (e.g. 'read') is at the end of the form, and all inflectional markers are prefixes; but the subject prefixes are close to the lexical part and preceded by other prefixes, so that they appear in the middle of the form. Here is 'be reading' with the forms divided into morphemes and the subject prefixes underlined:[5]

1sg.	(*shí*) *'ííníshta'* 'I am reading'	/'i-yí-ni-sh-ł-ta'/[6]
2sg.	(*ni*) *'ííníłta'* 'you (sg.) are reading'	/'i-yí-ni-'-ł-ta'/
3sg.	(*bí, hó*, etc.) *'ółta'*	/'i-yí-o-0-ł-ta'/
1pl.	(*nihí*) *'ííníilta'*	/'i-yí-ni-iid-ł-ta'/
2pl.	(*nihí*) *'íínółta'*	/'i-yí-ni-oh-ł-ta'/
3pl.	(*bí, hó*, etc.) *'ółta'*	/'i-yí-o-0-ł-ta'/

These four languages have subject-verb agreement in all verb forms except infinitives and participles (which we'll discuss much later). In the first three there are even plural imperative forms for telling more than one person to do something. English and Mandarin are very different. In English only the 3rd person singular is marked on verbs other than 'be' (see Lesson 14), and only in the present tense; compare the English present and past of *read* with the Spanish and Latin paradigms above:

		present	past
1sg.	*I*	*read* (pronounced "reed")	*read* ("red")[7]
2sg.	*you*	*read*	*read*
3sg.	*he / she / my grandfather /* etc.	*reads*	*read*
1pl.	*we*	*read*	*read*
2pl.	*you*	*read*	*read*
3pl.	*they / grandfathers /* etc.	*read*	*read*

---

[5] This paradigm is different from the ones in the preceding lessons not only because it indicates action going on (now), but also because it has an indefinite object; it means 'to read (something)', not 'to read (it/them)'. See the following lesson for further discussion.

[6] On the irregular appearance of /-o-/ in this paradigm see Kari 1976: 23.

[7] This is a graphic indication of how grossly inadequate English spelling is; almost every other language has a better system. See further Lesson 29.

This is very unusual. If the subject-verb agreement system of a language is minimal, it's usually the 3sg. of the present tense that has *no* inflectional marking – but that's the one form that does have a marker in English!

Mandarin is more typical in having no subject-verb agreement at all:

	singular	plural
1st	*wǒ kàn* 我看	*wǒmen kàn* 我们看
1st & 2nd	–	*zánmen kàn* 咱们看
2nd	*nǐ kàn* 你看	*nǐmen kàn* 你们看
3rd	*tā / wǒ yéye / etc. kàn* 他/我爺爺/…看	*tāmen / yéye / etc. kàn* 他们/爺爺/…看

Exercise

Here is a verb paradigm from an unfamiliar language. Does that language have subject-verb agreement? If it does, where are the agreement markers on the verb? What is each marker's function?

mimi ninasoma	'I am reading'
wewe unasoma	'you (sg.) are reading'
yeye anasoma	'(s)he is reading'
sisi tunasoma	'we are reading'
ninyi mnasoma	'you (pl.) are reading'
wao wanasoma	'they are reading'

Here is a verb paradigm from another unfamiliar language. Answer the same questions about it.

nemehka	'I find it'
kemehka	'you (sg.) find it'
mehkamwa	'(s)he finds it'
nemehkaapena	'we (not including you) find it'
kemehkaapena	'you and I find it'
kemehkaapwa	'you (pl.) find it'
mehkamooki	'they find it'
mehkaapi	'someone finds it'

To Be Remembered from Lesson 5

1 Pronouns are a special kind of noun phrase.

2 Every language has 1st-person pronouns meaning 'I' and 'we' and 2nd-person pronouns meaning 'you'.

3 3rd-person pronouns, like English 'he, she, it, they', are used to avoid repeating noun phrases that refer to the same person or thing.

4 In addition to expressing person and number, a language's pronoun system can make distinctions of many kinds, which differ greatly from language to language.

5 In languages that have subject-verb agreement, the person and number of the subject noun phrase (including subject pronouns) are marked on the verb. In some languages other characteristics of the subject are also marked on the verb; for instance, in Hebrew the gender of the subject is marked on the verb except in the 1st-person forms.

Further Reading

Quirk et al. 1980: 359–67 discuss the English system of subject-verb agreement in considerable detail, treating subjects conjoined by *and*, collective subjects, etc. You should consult a standard grammar of whatever language you are studying for its system of subject-verb agreement, if it has one; for instance, Butt and Benjamin 2011: 196–98 lay out the full conjugation of Spanish regular verbs.

6 | Direct Objects; Case

Other than subjects, what are noun phrases used for? To begin to answer that question we need to say a bit more about verbs.

Some verbs tell you what's going on in a clause without any additional specification. A typical English example is *rise*. We say *hot air rises*, and that's a complete clause (subject plus verb) without saying anything further. You *can* say something further if you want to – for instance, you can say how high something rose (*the balloon rose 300 feet*), or you can specify a location (*rose along the cliff* or *rose to the top*) – but you don't have to. Most importantly, if you try to ask a question like

>   *Hot air rises what?*
> or   *What does hot air rise?*
> or   *What got risen?*

your question will be meaningless. When something *rises*, it doesn't *rise something else*; it just goes up. In other words, *rise* cannot have a DIRECT OBJECT; there is nothing that "gets risen." A verb that cannot have a direct object is said to be INTRANSITIVE.

By contrast, a verb that normally does have a direct object is said to be TRANSITIVE. An English verb very similar to *rise* in meaning, but transitive, is *raise*. It's very difficult to produce a grammatical clause with the verb *raise* but no direct object. You can say

> *We raised it about two meters.*

with *it* as the direct object of *raised*, but you can't say

> **We raised about two meters.*

with no direct object. Nor can you say

> **It raised about two meters.*

(At least I can't say that.)

For any verb X, the direct object is whatever gets Xed (or got Xed, or will get Xed); sometimes it's more natural to say that it's whatever is (or was, or will be) Xed, but the point is the same. Note that once again we define "direct object" in terms of the sentence's structure, not by reference to the real-world (or imaginary) situation that it describes, for the same reasons that we defined "subject" that way.

In every language a very large number of verbs are transitive and normally have direct objects, and (as you've probably guessed) direct objects are always noun phrases. Here are some sentences you have seen before, this time with the direct objects underlined:

E   *The students read fifteen books.*
S   *Los estudiantes leyeron quince libros.*
L   *Discipulī quīndecim librōs lēgērunt.*
H   *Qārə'ū hattalmīđīm ḥ^amiššā 'āśār səp̄ārīm.*
N   *'Ółta'í 'ashdla'áadah naaltsoos yiyííłta'.*
M   *Xuésheng kàn le shíwǔ běn shū.*   学生看了十五本书.

So also:

E   *My grandfather is buying a coat.*
S   *Mi abuelo compra un abrigo.*
L   *Avus meus togam emit.*
H   *Qōne 'aḃ 'āḃī śalmā.*
N   *Shihanálí 'éétsoh nayiiniih.*
M   *Wǒ yéye mǎi yí jiàn dàyī.*   我爷爷买一件大衣.

Fifteen books are what got read; *a coat* is what is being bought: so those are the direct objects.

In most languages the direct object usually appears later in the clause than the subject. In English, Spanish, and Mandarin, it typically follows the verb; in Latin and Navajo it typically precedes the verb, because the verb is typically last, but it still follows the subject; in Hebrew, which places the verb first, it likewise follows the subject. (But see further below.)

Hebrew has a further device for marking direct objects: if the direct object is DEFINITE, it is introduced by *'et*. A definite noun phrase is one that the speaker expects the listener to know about already. In some languages, such as English, Spanish, and Hebrew, definite noun phrases are introduced by a definite ARTICLE (English *the*, Spanish *el*, Hebrew *ha-*; articles will be discussed further in Lesson 23). So if, instead of saying 'my grandfather is buying *a* coat', we wanted to say 'my grandfather is buying *the* coat', in Hebrew that would be:

H   *Qōne 'ab 'ābī 'et haśśalmā.*

with the direct object preceded both by *'et* and by the definite article.

In Spanish and Latin, and to a lesser extent in English, pronouns often have different forms depending on whether they are subjects or direct objects. Consider the following pairs of sentences:

E   *I love you.*   *You love me.*
S   *(Yo) te amo.*   *(Tú) me amas.*
L   *(Ego) tē amō.*   *(Tū) mē amās.*

Personal pronouns are always definite, because the listener already knows who they refer to, so we might expect that Hebrew object pronouns have to be preceded by *'et*, and they often are, but the pronoun is combined into a single word with *'et*, and the combinations are very different from their component parts:

'Āhabtī 'ōt-əkā. 'I love you.'   *'Āhabtā 'ōt-ī.* 'You love me.'

However, the same suffixes (sometimes in slightly different form) can be attached directly to the verb, e.g.:

'Ahabtī-kā. 'I love you.'   *'Ahabta-nī.* 'You love me.'

Mandarin pronouns do not change their shape, regardless of their function in the clause:

M   *Wǒ ài nǐ.* 我爱你.   'I love you.'   *Nǐ ài wǒ.* 你爱我.   'You love me.'

On Navajo pronoun objects, see below.

Using different forms for subject and object (and other functions) is called CASE-MARKING. In English and Spanish (and French and Italian) only pronouns are case-marked – although there is a further complication for Spanish direct objects, which appears below and will be dealt with more fully in the following lesson. In Latin, however, all nouns are also case-marked; every noun in the language has several different forms for use in different functions in the clause. Consider the following pairs of sentences:

E   *The dog is chasing the man.*   *The man is chasing the dog.*
S   *El perro caza al hombre.*   *El hombre caza al perro.*
L   *Canis hominem persequitur.*   *Homō__ canem persequitur.*[1]

Unless the subject or the direct object is a pronoun, English distinguishes them only by their position in the clause. Spanish additionally marks direct objects that refer to people or animals by preceding them with *a* (and *a el* contracts to *al*). Latin distinguishes all subjects and direct objects by case markers, usually called "CASE endings" because they are the last part of the noun. Because case-marking is so pervasive in Latin (and many other languages), there is a terminology for discussing it. The form used for subjects is called the NOMINATIVE CASE; the form used for direct objects is called the ACCUSATIVE CASE. In our sample sentences *ego* 'I', *tū* 'you (sg.)', *homō* 'person', and *canis* 'dog' are all nominative, while *mē*, *tē*, *hominem*, and *canem* are the corresponding accusatives.

Unlike our other sample languages, Navajo has not only subject-verb agreement, but also object-verb agreement; the direct object is marked on the verb. It might even be more accurate to say that the direct object pronoun has been INCORPORATED into the verb. For that reason, independent pronouns are hardly ever

---

[1] In spite of the way elementary Latin grammars sometimes present the paradigm of 'person, man', the nom. sg. *homō* has a zero ending, before which the normal stem *homin-* is replaced by *homō-*. All other forms are built to the stem *homin-* with normal consonant-stem endings; *-in-* is not part of the endings.

used to express direct objects. Here are the sentences 'I love you' and 'you love me' in Navajo (note that *'ayóí* is an adverb meaning 'very much'):

N   *(Shí) 'ayóí 'ánósh'ní.*   'I love you.'   /'á-ni-yí-o-sh-d-ní/
    (Ni) 'ayóí 'áshííní'ní.   'You love me.'   /'á-shi-yí-ni-'-d-ní/

(The object markers in this partial paradigm are /-shi-/ 'me' and /-ni-/ 'you', which lose their vowels and contract with following verbal prefixes; the subject markers are /-sh-/ 'I' and a high tone indicating 'you' which "docks" on an immediately preceding vowel.) In addition to Athabaskan languages (the language family to which Navajo belongs), other languages that have object-verb agreement and/or incorporation of an object pronoun into the verb include Eskimo-Aleut languages, the Algonkian languages of northeastern North America, the Bantu languages of central and southern Africa, and Georgian. All those languages also have subject-verb agreement; there seem to be no languages that have *only* object-verb agreement. Evidently subjects are special.

If a language is heavily case-marked, like Latin, the most straightforward way to mark the cases would be to have a single ending for each case, different from the plural ending(s). Turkish does exactly that. For instance, in Turkish *ev* is 'house', plural *evler* 'houses'; the locative is *evde* 'in the house' or 'at home', and the locative plural *evlerde* 'in the houses'. Such a system is called AGGLUTINATIVE; the idea is that you glue the pieces together and add up the meanings, as straightforwardly as possible.

What's surprising is that Latin and many other languages don't have an agglutinative inflectional system. Number and case are marked together by single FUSED endings (so called because you can't analyze them into a piece that marks number and another that marks case). For instance, 'grandfather', 'toga', 'person', 'dog' are marked as follows in the nominative and accusative:

		'grandfather'	'toga'	'person'	'dog'
sg.	nom.	*avus*	*toga*	*homō*	*canis*
	acc.	*avum*	*togam*	*hominem*	*canem*
pl.	nom.	*avī*	*togae*	*hominēs*	*canēs*
	acc.	*avōs*	*togās*	*hominēs*	*canēs*

As you can see, the system is complex, idiosyncratic, and not always unambiguous (note that the nom. and acc. pl. are the same for some nouns; for some others even the nom. and acc. sg. are the same). The fused case-and-number endings are one of the complications that make learning Latin comparatively difficult. On the other hand, because Latin does not rely entirely on word order to distinguish subjects and direct objects, they can be shifted around for emphasis; in addition to

Canis hominem persequitur.

you can also say

Hominem canis persequitur. (some emphasis on *hominem:* the dog isn't chasing something else)

as well as

Hominem persequitur canis. (heavy emphasis on *canis:* it's the *dog* that's chasing the man!)

– and they all mean that the dog is chasing the man, not the other way round.

Let's return to transitive verbs and their direct objects. In many languages a transitive verb can be used without any direct object, even an implied one. We saw that that wasn't possible for *raise* in English. But it is possible for *lift:*

We lifted about two meters, and that was enough.

In this sentence it's clear enough that something or other must have been lifted, but the speaker isn't saying what and doesn't necessarily even care whether the hearer can figure it out; the focus is entirely on the action of lifting. That is especially common with verbs like *eat.* Compare the following two sets of sentences:

E	*They ate the lunch.*[2]	*Have you eaten?*
S	*Comieron el almuerzo.*	*Ha comido usted?*
L	*Prandium ēdērunt.*	*Ēdistīne?*
M	*Tāmen chī le wǔfàn.* 他们吃了午饭.	*Nǐ chī le ma?* 你吃了吗?

---

[2] A lunch that has already been mentioned (hence the definite article – see above). I use precisely this example because in Spanish and Latin there are verbs meaning 'have lunch'; the normal ways of saying 'they ate lunch' are *almorzaron* and *prandērunt* respectively.

In the first set, in which the direct objects are underlined, the speaker is saying that some people ate a particular thing. In the second set the speaker doesn't know what, if anything, the addressee ate, and it doesn't matter; the speaker is really asking, 'Are you hungry?', implying an offer of food. Hebrew can likewise use 'eat' with no object at all, e.g. in *I Kings* 18.41:

Wayyōmer 'Ēliyyāhū lə 'Aḥ'ā ḇ, "ˁlē, ˁḵōl ūšəṯē, kī-qōl hᵃmōn haggāšem.
'Eliah said to Ahab, "Go up, <u>eat and drink</u>, for (there is) the sound of lots of rain."'

However, Navajo makes the difference between transitive verbs with and without objects explicit, because direct objects must be marked on the verb:

Yíníyą́ą́'? 'Have you eaten it?'   vs.   *Ííníyą́ą́'?* 'Have you eaten?'

The second verb form means, literally, 'Have you eaten anything?', with indefinite direct object *'i-* 'something'.

You can describe this situation by saying that lots of verbs in lots of languages (though not in all) can be used both as transitives and as intransitives. It's probably more complicated than that: even if it's clear that the direct object can be omitted, it's easier to do with some verbs than with others, and there might be different reasons for omitting the object which should be treated differently. But the most important thing to remember is that some details of grammar are rigid while others can be flexible. Subject-verb agreement is usually rigid; transitivity is flexible in many languages, but if a verb does have a direct object, its case-marking is usually rigid; and so on.

Also, if there are null-subject languages, are there null-object languages that can omit an object pronoun even when it refers to something already in the discourse? Some languages do omit some object pronouns, but the rules differ considerably from language to language. Mandarin usually omits the 3rd-person pronoun *tā* when it's a direct object referring to a thing, but not when it refers to a person, e.g. (examples from Yip and Rimmington 1997: 20–21):

Zhèi běn xiǎoshuō hěn cháng, kěshi wǒ hěn xǐhuan __.
这本小说很长,可是我很喜欢__.
'This novel (is) very long, but I very much like <u>it</u>.'

(the pronoun would go where the blank is), but:

> *Nèi ge rén hěn jiāo'ào, kěshì wǒ hěn xǐhuan tā.*
> 那个人很骄傲, 可是我很喜欢他.
> 'This person (is) very proud, but I very much like him/her.'

Latin omits 3rd-person direct object pronouns much more widely if they can be inferred from the context; so does Hebrew, e.g. in *Genesis* 3.12:

> *Hī nāṯǝnā-lī   min-hā'ēṣ   wā'ōḵēl.*
> '*She* gave (it) to me from the tree, and I ate (it).'

Navajo and English do not omit pronouns referring to specific things in the context, and Spanish does not seem to either.

Exercise

Identify the direct objects in the following sentences, as well as places where direct objects have been omitted.

1. *I've never seen the Taj Mahal, and I regret it.*
2. *Why did they disturb the aardvark? Didn't they know?*
3. *Don't elect a buffoon; the country can't survive that.*
4. *By the time I get to London I'll be completely exhausted.*
5. *I can hear the animal out there, but I can't see it.*
6. *I'll come get you.*
7. *Disregard all those irrelevant bits of information.*
8. *I don't have time to do that.*

To Be Remembered from Lesson 6

1 In every language many verbs, called transitive verbs, take direct objects; for any verb X, the direct object is whatever gets Xed (or got Xed, or will get Xed).

2 Many transitive verbs can be used with or without a direct object; the verb meaning 'eat' is usually such a verb.

3 Even when a direct object is present, some languages do not have to express it, while others do; that is like the difference between null-subject languages and others, although it is more complicated.

4 Languages have a variety of ways of marking the direct object, including word order, case-marking, and markers like Hebrew 'eṭ.

5 Some case-marking languages are agglutinative, with a separate marker for noun plurals and for each case; others have fused markers.

6 If a language uses case-marking extensively, it is possible to put the words in many different orders without changing the relations beween subject and direct object.

Further Reading

Quirk et al. 1980: 348–49 give a series of definitions that is relevant to this lesson and the next two. Butt and Benjamin 2011: 154–65 and 328–35 discuss in detail the Spanish system of marking objects. Gildersleeve and Lodge 1895: 207–23, 240–42 detail the case-marking of objects in Latin (relevant to the next lesson as well as this one), with various irregularities depending on the specific verb involved. Pinkster 2015, ch. 4 is an in-depth discussion of Latin subjects and objects from a modern perspective; ch. 12 deals with case-marking and prepositional phrases. (Both chapters are relevant to the next lesson as well.) Young and Morgan 1980, grammar pp. 169–85, describe the Navajo system of direct object markers.

7 | Double-Object Verbs

Some verbs commonly have two objects. The most important group are verbs like *give* and *tell*. Consider the following sentences:

E   *Dad gave me the book. | Dad gave the book to me.*
S   *Papá me dio el libro.*
L   *Pater mihi librum dedit.*
H[1] *Nātan lī 'ābī 'eṯ hassēp̄er.*
N   *Shizhé'é naaltsoos shaa ní'ą́.*
M   *Bàba gěi le wǒ shū.*

In these sentences *the book* (*| el libro | librum | 'eṯ hassēp̄er | naaltsoos | shū*) is what got given – what got transferred to me – so that's the direct object, and I've underlined it. But there is a second object, *(to) me* (*| me | mihi | lī | shaa | wǒ*), which I've marked with dotted underlining. It's a different kind of object, because I didn't get transferred; rather, the direct object was transferred *to* me. An object to or for which the direct object got Xed (for any verb X) is called an INDIRECT OBJECT.

Different languages mark indirect objects in different ways. In Latin they have a caseform of their own, the DATIVE case. As you can see in the above

---

[1] In this sentence *lī* 'to me' immediately follows the verb, preceding the subject, because it is unstressed.

example, the indirect object *mihi* has a different form from the (accusative) direct object *mē*, and all the pronouns have special dative forms. Here are the noun paradigms discussed in the last lesson with dative forms added:

		'grandfather'	'toga'	'person'	'dog'
sg.	nom.	*avus*	*toga*	*homō*	*canis*
	acc.	*avum*	*togam*	*hominem*	*canem*
	dat.	*avō*	*togae*	*hominī*	*canī*
pl.	nom.	*avī*	*togae*	*hominēs*	*canēs*
	acc.	*avōs*	*togās*	*hominēs*	*canēs*
	dat.	*avīs*	*togīs*	*hominibus*	*canibus*

(I do realize that even the Romans didn't usually give things to togas, but the forms are regular and easy to construct.) This is typical of languages with pervasive case-marking.

Mandarin simply puts the indirect object between the verb and the direct object, and that's also one way of doing it in English. Spanish has special forms, sg. *le* and pl. *les*, for 3rd-person pronouns that are indirect objects; otherwise the distinction between direct and indirect objects is complexly marked. (See further below.)

Hebrew and Navajo use ADPOSITIONS to indicate indirect objects, and English can do so. Like verbs, adpositions have objects. In Hebrew the adposition is a PREPOSITION, because it precedes its object: *lī* is literally *l+ī* 'to-me'. In Navajo the adposition is a POSTPOSITION, because it follows its object: *shaa* is literally *sh+aa* 'me-to'.

English is somewhat unusual in having two options for marking indirect objects. In addition to the fact that one uses the preposition *to* and the other doesn't, there is a fixed difference in word order between the two constructions: when the indirect object has no preposition to introduce it, it is placed first, but otherwise the direct object usually is. There is a similar alternation between the two options with various other verbs; with some (such as *tell*) the preposition is also *to*, but with others it is *for*, e.g.:

> *Mom painted her a picture.*
> *Mom painted a picture for her.*

Latin and Mandarin have no adpositional option for indirect objects, while Hebrew and Navajo always use an adposition.

The Spanish system is much more complex. If the indirect object is a pronoun, it usually precedes the verb and is not accompanied by any other word, as in the example above. You can use the preposition *a* 'to' with a pronominal indirect object, but only for emphasis – and you have to use the non-prepositional option too, doubling up the pronoun:

> *Papá me dio el libro a mí.*   'Dad gave the book to *me*.'
> (Dad me gave the book to me)

Indirect objects that are full noun phrases (as opposed to mere pronouns) are always marked with *a* – but you still need to use a (completely redundant) unstressed pronoun:

> *Papá le dio el libro a Juan.*   'Dad gave John the book / gave the book to John.'
>
> (Dad him gave the book to John)
> *Mamá le pintó una pintura a mi hermana.*
> 'Mom painted my sister a picture / painted a picture for my sister.'

Moreover, direct objects are also marked with *a* if they refer to human beings or animals:

> *Busco a mi amigo.*   'I'm looking for my friend.'
> *Busco mi ordenador.*   'I'm looking for my computer.'

We don't need to examine the Spanish system in further detail; the point is that it's more complex than those of our other sample languages, and therefore difficult for foreigners to learn.

As so often, Chinese languages do things somewhat differently. Mandarin has no case-marking and does not use adpositions to introduce indirect objects, so with the verb *gěi* 'give' the indirect object is marked by the fact that it immediately follows the verb, as in the English non-prepositional option. But if the indirect object depends on some other verb, *gěi* must be inserted to GOVERN it as an object:

> *Māma gěi wǒ huà le yì fú huà.* 妈妈给我画了一幅画.
> (Mom give me paint COMPLETIVE one CLASSIFIER painting)
> 'Mom painted me a picture / painted a picture for me.'

This is part of a larger phenomenon that will be discussed further in Lesson 19: Mandarin often uses multiple verbs in a single clause.

While most double-object verbs govern a direct object and an indirect object, there are a few that govern *two* direct objects. Some are idiosyncratic to particular languages, but a very widespread type is verbs that mean *make X Y*, where *X* and *Y* refer to the same real-world entity. For instance, in the sentence

> *We elected Barack Obama president*

the noun phrases *Barack Obama* and *president* refer to the same person, and if you ask who got elected, both *Barack Obama* and *(a) president* are correct answers – so both are direct objects of *elected*. You would expect both to be in the accusative case in Latin, and that turns out to be true:

> *Quirītēs Iūlium Caesarem cōnsulem creāvērunt.*
> 'The citizens of Rome elected Julius Caesar consul.'

As you may have noticed from the table on the second page of this lesson, Latin nouns in the accusative singular tend to end in *-m*, and, sure enough, both *Iūlium Caesarem* and *cōnsulem* are in the accusative.

Exercise

Consider the following sentences in an unfamiliar language (data from Baker 1988a, 1988b):

Mbidzi zinapatsa msampha kwa nkhandwe.
'The zebras gave the trap to the fox.'
Mbidzi zinapatsa nkhandwe msampha.
'The zebras gave the fox the trap.'
Mbidzi zinapereka mpiringidzo kwa mtsikana.
'The zebras handed the crowbar to the girl.'
Mbidzi zinaperekera mtsikana mpiringidzo.
'The zebras handed the girl the crowbar.'

Agalu anatumiza nsomba kwa fisi.
'The dogs sent some fish to the hyena.'
Agalu anatumizira fisi nsomba.
'The dogs sent the hyena some fish.'
Mvuu zinalemba kalata kwa amalinyero.
'The hippos wrote a letter to the sailors.'
Mvuu zinalembera amalinyero kalata.
'The hippos wrote the sailors a letter.'

How does this language mark indirect objects? What grammatical device that you have *not* seen in this lesson does this language have? (You won't have a term for it, but you should be able to isolate its marker; you might or might not be able to guess its exact function.)

To Be Remembered from Lesson 7

1 Verbs that mean things like 'give', 'tell', and 'make (something for someone)' typically take two objects. One is the direct object. The other, denoting the person to whom something is given or told or for whom something is made, is called the indirect object.

2 Languages have a variety of ways of marking indirect objects – roughly the same range of ways as for direct objects, with differences in detail.

3 Verbs that mean things like 'make (something into something else)' also take two objects, but in this case the objects refer to the same entity, and both are direct objects.

8 | "Linking" Verbs; Adjectives

There are clauses that include a verb and two noun phrases in which neither noun phrase is an object. The verbs in those clauses are verbs like *be*, *become*, and *seem*, which state some kind of equation between the noun phrases: that is, they state that the subject is, or becomes, or seems to be the same as some other entity. If you apply the direct object test to clauses like these, it usually doesn't work. For example:

> *Barack Obama is the president.* (question: *What gets been?)
> *Thomas Merton became a monk.* (question: *What got become?)

The questions simply make no sense, because there is no direct object.

In a language like Latin, in which subjects are in the nominative case, you would expect these COMPLEMENT noun phrases to be in the nominative too, and in fact they are:

> *Iūlius Caesar__ cōnsul__ est.*   'Julius Caesar is consul.'
> *Ossa lapis fīunt.*   'The bones become stone.'
>   (Ovid, *Metamorphoses* IV.660)

(The nominative endings are underlined.)

In Spanish, in which the 1st- and 2nd-person singular pronouns are clearly marked for case, you would expect to find the subject forms used as complements, and Spanish does so:[1]

El feo de la foto eres tú.   'The ugly one in the photo is you.'
¿Quién ha dicho eso? – Ha sido yo. 'Who said that?' – 'It was I.'

In English we might expect to find the same for the first and non-neuter 3rd-person pronouns, which mark case (subject *I, we, he, she, they* vs. object *me, us, him, her, them*), and in formal English we are supposed to say *it is I, it was she*, and so on. But the English case system has been evolving in a different direction for a long time, and in colloquial English it's normal to say *it's me, it was her*, etc., as if the pronouns were objects.

Clauses like these have an obvious relation to the last type of double-object verbs discussed in the preceding lesson. In the Latin example adduced there,

Quirītēs Iūlium Caesarem cōnsulem creāvērunt.
'The citizens of Rome elected Julius Caesar consul.'

both objects are in the accusative because they are equated and they are objects; in the Latin example adduced above,

Iūlius Caesar__ cōnsul__ est.   'Julius Caesar is consul.'

both noun phrases are in the nominative because they are equated and one is the subject. (There is a roughly similar relationship between the indirect object and direct object of *give* and the subject and direct object of *have:* the indirect object of the former corresponds to the subject of the latter.)

These "linking" verbs can also be followed by ADJECTIVES, words which refer to qualities rather than entities. In Latin, in which adjectives are inflected for case, gender, and number, adjectives in complement position are in the nominative too, and they agree in gender and number with the subject. Spanish and English do not inflect adjectives for case, but Spanish does inflect them for gender and

---

[1] These examples are from Butt and Benjamin 2011: 137.

number, and a Spanish complement agrees in gender and number with its subject except in special cases:[2]

   E *Our grandfathers are old.*   *Our grandmothers are respectable.*

   S *Nuestros abuelos son viejos.* *Nuestras abuelas son venerandas.*

   L *Avī nostrī senēs sunt.*   *Aviae nostrae venerandae sunt.*

Spanish also has a further complication that the other languages do not. There are two verbs meaning 'be' in Spanish. Roughly speaking, *ser* indicates identity, whereas *estar* indicates condition or location. One result is that *ser* is almost always used when the complement of the verb is a noun phrase, including pronouns; in the examples with pronouns above, *eres* and *ha sido* are forms of *ser*. With adjective complements the situation is more complex. *Ser* is usually used to indicate inherent conditions. Thus in the Spanish examples above *son* is a form of *ser*, because grandfathers are inherently old and we are asserting that our grandmothers are unalterably respectable. But it is possible to say

   Nuestros abuelos están viejos.

and that would mean

   'Our grandfathers have grown old.'

Thus *estar* can be used to indicate a change of state. It is also used for most temporary, or at least non-inherent, conditions. Thus one would say

   Nuestros abuelos están cansados.
   'Our grandfathers are tired.'

We don't need to go into further detail here; for a full description of the system, which involves a number of idiosyncratic exceptions, see Butt and Benjamin 2011: 408–16.

   Since Chinese languages have no inflection, one would expect the corresponding sentences in Mandarin to be much like those of English, but that is only partly true. It is true if the complement is a noun phrase:

---

[2] As you can see, 'our', which is part of the noun phrases headed by 'grandmothers' and 'grandfathers', also agrees in gender and number with the noun in Spanish and Latin; see further Lessons 11 and 22.

E   *We are teachers.*
S   *Somos maestros.*
L   *Doctōrēs sumus.*
M   *Wǒmen shì lǎoshī.* 我们是老师.

But if the complement is an adjective, no linking verb is used:

E   *Our grandfathers are old.*
M   *Wǒmen yéye hěn lǎo.* 我们爺爺很老.

The word *hěn* in this sentence is not a verb; it's an adverb meaning 'very' or 'a lot'. It turns out that in Mandarin an adjective by itself cannot be a complement; thus the adjective *lǎo* 'old' must be preceded by *hěn*, which in this context has been "bleached" of its usual meaning. Moreover, if an adjective refers to a quality that cannot be more or less, it has to be bracketed by *shì … de:*[3]

Zhè shì zhēn de.   这是真的.   'This is true.'
Tāde chènshān shì bái de.   他的衬衫是白的.   'His shirt is white.'

(For much more information on the syntax of Mandarin adjectives, see Huang 2016.) You can see that the total absence of inflection, although it does simplify Chinese grammar, does not make the language simple or easy to learn; you also need to take account of the rules of syntax, and Chinese syntax is not particularly simple. As we will see in subsequent lessons, the same can be said of English.

Hebrew expresses equations of this kind somewhat differently. In Biblical Hebrew the verb 'be' is often unexpressed; in the present tense it is regularly omitted. Thus, in *Psalm* 24:

Mī ze melek hakkābōd? – Hū melek hakkābōd.
'Who[4] (is) king of glory?' – 'He (is) king of glory.'

If the complement is an adjective, it is usually placed first; thus

Ṭōbā hā'āreṣ.
(good the-land)

---

[3] These examples are from Yip and Rimmington 1997: 32.

[4] Literally 'who this', with *ze* 'this' used to focus the interrogative pronoun; see Gesenius and Kautzsch 1910: 442. An alternative translation is 'Who is it that is …' (Aaron Rubin, p.c.).

is the usual way of saying 'The land is good.' (Note that the adjective agrees in gender and number with the subject, as in Spanish; *'ereṣ* 'land' is feminine in Hebrew.) Even in a sequence of clauses referring to the past the verb 'be' will be expressed in the first and omitted in the others; an example is *Genesis 1.2*:

Wəhā'āreṣ,   hāyəṯā ṯōhū wāḇōhū, wəḥōšeḵ __ 'al-pənē ṯəhōm,
'And (as for) the earth, it was waste and void, and darkness (was) over the abyss,
wərūᵃḥ ᵉlōhīm __ məraḥep̄eṯ 'al-pənē hammāyim.
and the spirit of God (was) hovering over the waters.'

  Navajo has no adjectives; instead it has STATIVE verbs, which express states in much the same way as adjectives. For instance, there are verbs meaning 'be good', 'be small', etc. which translate the phrases 'be + (adjective)' of other languages straightforwardly:

   'Asdzání nineez. 'The woman is tall.'
   (Shí) nishneez. 'I am tall.' (*-sh-* 'I')
   'Áłchíní niłyázhí. 'The child is little.' / 'The children are little.'
   (Nihí) nółyázhí. 'You (pl.) are little.' (*-o(h)-* 'you (pl.)')

Navajo does have a verb *'á ... t'é* meaning 'be', but it is used only with noun phrase complements, e.g.:

   Díí shizhé'é 'át'é. 'This (*díí*) is my father.'

  Finally, I should point out that the discussion of this lesson is incomplete. I've been talking about adjectives used as complements of linking verbs, but it must have occurred to you that they can be used in noun phrases too; that is, you can say not only *the grass is green*, but also *the green grass*. That use of adjectives will be discussed in Lesson 22.

Exercise

Here are some forms and phrases from an unfamiliar language. Do you think the word that means 'red' is more likely to be an adjective or a stative verb? Why?

nemeškosi 'I am red'
kemeškosipena 'you and I are red'

meškosiwa '(s)he is red'

ahkohkwa meškosiwa 'the kettle is red'

nepi meškwaawi 'the water is red'

Here are some sentences from another unfamiliar language. Does this language require adjective complements to agree with their subjects in gender and number (like Spanish and Latin, for example)? State the evidence for your answer.

Hē tʰúrā iskʰūrā́ estin. 'The door is strong.'

Ho neāníās iskʰūròs egéneto. 'The young man has become strong.'

Hoi emoì adelpʰoì iskʰūroí eisin. 'My brothers are strong.'

Hē métēr hē hūmetérā iskʰūrā́ estin. 'Your (pl.) mother is strong.'

Hai nêͅes iskʰūraí eisin. 'The ships are strong.'

Tò paidíon iskʰūrón esti par' elpídas. 'The child is unexpectedly strong.'

To Be Remembered from Lesson 8

1 Verbs that mean things like 'be', 'become', and 'seem' do not have direct objects; they express an equation between the subject and another phrase, which is called a complement.

2 Complements can be noun phrases or adjectives.

3 If a language has case-marking, the complement will usually be in the same case as the subject. If a language requires its adjectives to agree with their nouns in number and/or gender, there will usually be such agreement between the subject and an adjective complement.

4 Some languages omit the verb 'be' in some circumstances.

5 Some languages have stative verbs instead of adjectives.

Further Reading

Young and Morgan 1980, grammar pp. 289–306 is a fascinating discussion and illustration of Navajo stative verbs. Although their grammar is peculiar to Athabaskan languages, their meanings are representative of stative verbs in other languages as well.

9 | Personal Pronoun Systems

We discussed pronouns in Lessons 5, 6, and 7 in the context of their relationships to verbs. This lesson will present the PERSONAL PRONOUNS of our languages individually in detail, with the aim of showing how each *system* is structured. (Personal pronouns are the ones that primarily indicate person and number; there are other, less central kinds of pronoun which we can deal with later.)

Mandarin and Navajo have the simplest systems. To recapitulate what was said in Lesson 5, the Mandarin system distinguishes only person and number, and the marking of number is regular, in fact agglutinative:

	1st	1st & 2nd	2nd	3rd
singular	*wǒ* 我	–	*nǐ* 你	*tā* 他
plural	*wǒmen* 我们	*zánmen* 咱们	*nǐmen* 你们	*tāmen* 他们

Not all native speakers of Mandarin use *zánmen*; some substitute *wǒmen*, using the 1st-person form when both 1st and 2nd persons are referenced, as in many other languages. The only detail not noted in the above chart is that there is a special polite 2sg. form (only), namely *nín* 您, which stands somewhat outside the system. The Navajo system is different but also very simple:

	1st	2nd	3rd default	3rd animate
singular	*shí*	*ni*	*bí*	*hó*
plural	*nihí*	*nihí*	*bí*	*hó*
distributive	*danihí*	*danihí*	*daabí*	*daahó*

Plural is marked only for the 1st and 2nd persons, but 1pl. and 2pl. are not distinguished. Marking of distributive 'each' is basically agglutinative.

The English system is not as simple, but it is not very complex. English distinguishes subject forms from object forms, and in the 3rd person it distinguishes three genders, masculine, feminine, and neuter, in the singular:

		1st	2nd	3rd masc.	3rd fem.	3rd neut.
sg.	subj.	*I*	*you*	*he*	*she*	*it*
	obj.	*me*	*you*	*him*	*her*	*it*
pl.	subj.	*we*	*you*		*they*	
	obj.	*us*	*you*		*them*	

The 3rd-person singular forms reference "natural" gender: the masculine forms are used only for male persons and animals (and entities thought of as masculine, such as God), the feminine forms only for female persons and animals, and the neuter forms for everything else. (The more arbitrary gender systems of other languages will be discussed in Lesson 12.)

Several things about this system are noteworthy. The 1st-person forms are SUPPLETIVE; that is, they do not resemble one another and cannot be derived from a single "underlying" form. There is also suppletion among the 3rd-person forms, but somewhat less: the plural forms begin with *th-*, the masc. and fem. sg. forms with *h-*, and the neut. sg. form is different from both. In the 3pl. there is SYNCRETISM of genders: a single form is used for all three genders; in the neut. sg. there is syncretism between the subject and object forms (they are identical). All these peculiarities were inherited from earlier stages of English or from ancestors of English hundreds or even thousands of years ago.

In this idiosyncratic system the single 2nd-person form stands out like a sore thumb: it exhibits syncretism not only between subject and object forms but even between singular and plural, unlike all the other personal pronouns. It turns out that that is a fairly recent innovation. What happened was the following. Originally there were four 2nd-person forms, parallel to the 1st-person forms:

	1st	2nd
sg. subj.	*I*	*thou*
obj.	*me*	*thee*
pl. subj.	*we*	*ye*
obj.	*us*	*you*

Shakespeare, writing about 400 years ago, still uses all four forms in their original functions. But a slow change had already begun more than two centuries before. Imitating French, speakers of English had begun to use the plural *ye* and *you* for politeness in place of *thou* and *thee*. In Chaucer's works that usage is still inconsistent; by Shakespeare's time it was normal. In addition, a generation or so before Shakespeare was born, people began to replace the subject form *ye* with *you*, again inconsistently. Sometime in the eighteenth century both processes went to completion, leaving *you* as the only 2nd-person pronoun in normal speech.

The Spanish pronoun system is much more complex than that of English. In addition to distinguishing subject from object forms, Spanish also has stressed and unstressed object forms, and it distinguishes unstressed 3sg. direct objects from indirect objects. There is also a distinction between familiar and polite 2nd-person forms, and various forms distinguish gender (masculine, feminine, and neuter). The whole system can be tabulated as follows:

| | | o b j e c t | | |
| | | unstressed | | stressed |
	subject	direct	indirect	
1sg.	*yo*	*me*	*me*	*mí*
1pl. masc.	*nosotros*	*nos*	*nos*	*nosotros*
1pl. fem.	*nosotras*	*nos*	*nos*	*nosotras*
2sg. familiar	*tú*	*te*	*te*	*ti*
2pl. fam. masc.	*vosotros*	*os*	*os*	*vosotros*
2pl. fam. fem.	*vosotras*	*os*	*os*	*vosotras*
2sg. polite masc.	*usted*	*lo*	*le*	*usted*
2sg. polite fem.	*usted*	*la*	*le*	*usted*

2pl. polite masc.	*ustedes*	*los*	*les*	*ustedes*
2pl. polite fem.	*ustedes*	*las*	*les*	*ustedes*
3sg. masc.	*él*	*lo*	*le*	*él*
3sg. fem.	*ella*	*la*	*le*	*ella*
3pl. masc.	*ellos*	*los*	*les*	*ellos*
3pl. fem.	*ellas*	*las*	*les*	*ellas*
3sg. neut.	*ello*	*lo*	*le*	*ello*

As you can see, there are numerous syncretisms in this system – so many that it sometimes makes more sense to specify when forms are different from each other than when they are the same. In the next few paragraphs I will try to describe the system in a way that might make sense.

The unstressed object forms are used as objects of verbs; the stressed object forms are used as objects of prepositions. The stressed object forms are different from the subject forms in the 1sg. and the 2sg. familiar; *otherwise they are identical with the subject forms.*

Spanish pronouns distinguish gender *whenever they can.* Therefore they do so in the following instances:

1) all the 3rd-person forms *except* the unstressed indirect object, because in the other 3rd-person forms there is a potential distinction between masculine *-o(s)* (or zero ending) and feminine *-a(s)*;
2) the unstressed direct object forms for the 2nd person polite, because they are identical with the corresponding 3rd-person forms;
3) the stressed 1pl. and 2pl. familiar forms (including the subject forms), because they are really compounded with the adjective *otro* 'other', and adjectives distinguish gender in Spanish.

(Gender will be discussed in more detail in Lesson 12.) In addition, the normal noun and adjective plural marker *-(e)s* is found on all the plural pronouns. On the other hand, direct and indirect objects are not distinguished except in the 3rd person (and, therefore, in the 2nd person polite).

In Spanish, as in many other languages, unstressed words do not obey the same rules of word order as stressed words do. The unstressed object pronouns are usually placed *before* the verbs whose object they are, even though stressed objects follow the verb. The following examples are typical:

¿Me ves en la foto?	'Do you see me in the photo?'
Me lo dé, por favor.	'Give it to me, please.'
No lo puedo ver.	'I can't see him/it.'
Le dieron la carta.	'They gave the letter to him/her.'
La mira en el espejo.	'He/she is looking at her in the mirror.'

An exception are unstressed objects of imperatives. The verb in the second sentence above is actually a SUBJUNCTIVE – a form used for polite requests, among other things[1] – so the object pronouns precede the verb; but if you were talking to a small child you could use the imperative and say

> *Dámelo!*   'Give it to me!'

As we saw in Lesson 7, stressed objects indicating persons are preceded by the preposition *a*, but an unstressed object pronoun is also used, e.g.:

> *Nos visitan a nosotros.*   'They're visiting us.'

The Latin system is similar but in some ways simpler – except that Latin has five cases, and all the pronouns have to have forms for all five. The cases are nominative, accusative, genitive (typically translatable by English 'of', see Lesson 11), dative, and ablative (translatable by 'with', and also used after certain prepositions):

				3rd		
		1st	2nd	masc.	neut.	fem.
sg.	nom.	*ego*	*tū*	*is*	*id*	*ea*
	acc.	*mē*	*tē*	*eum*	*id*	*eam*
	gen.	*meī*	*tuī*		*e i u s*	
	dat.	*mihi*	*tibi*		*e ī*	
	abl.	*mē*	*tē*		*e ō*	*eā*
pl.	nom.	*nōs*	*vōs*	*eī*	*ea*	*eae*
	acc.	*nōs*	*vōs*	*eōs*	*ea*	*eās*
	gen.	*nostrī*	*vestrī*		*e ō r u m*	*eārum*
	dat.-abl.	*nōbīs*	*vōbīs*		*e ī s*	

These paradigms too exhibit a good many syncretisms. One is a fluke: it's just a historical accident that the accusative and ablative forms are identical in

---

[1] See Lesson 15 for more information on Spanish subjunctives.

the 1sg. and 2sg. But the syncretism between dative plural and ablative plural is systematic in Latin – *all* nouns, adjectives, and pronouns exhibit it. So is the syncretism between nom. and acc. sg. in neuters, and between nom. and acc. pl. in neuters. In addition, syncretism between nom. and acc. pl. even in non-neuters is common enough in Latin that it's no real surprise to find it in the 1pl. and 2pl. pronouns. But there is more. The 3rd-person pronoun is inflected like an adjective to a large degree in Latin, and it's a general rule that in the genitive, dative, and ablative cases (in both numbers) neuters are not different from masculines. The only real surprise is that in the gen. sg. and dat. sg. of the 3rd-person pronoun even the feminine is like the masculine – but that syncretism too recurs in the interrogative pronoun, for example (see Lesson 21).

Why all this syncretism? If the Latin inflectional system were agglutinative, like that of Turkish (see Lesson 5), syncretism would be severely dysfunctional, because it would obscure an otherwise clear system in which each inflectional marker meant something easily identifiable. But because Latin inflectional markers are fused, you have to memorize a large number of markers whose meanings are opaque and arbitrary – and in a system like that, syncretism reduces the burden on the learner's memory.

The Latin case system will be dealt with in more detail in Lesson 13.

The Biblical Hebrew system also resembles that of Spanish in a general way. The stressed forms, used for the subject when the verb is omitted (see Lesson 8) or for emphasis (see Lesson 5) are quite different from the unstressed forms used as the objects of prepositions or of 'e*ṯ* (see Lesson 6):

	stressed	unstressed (with 'ō*ṯ*-)
1sg.	'ānō*ḵ*ī, '*ᵃ*nī	-ī
2sg. masc.	'attā	-*ḵ*ā
2sg. fem.	'att	-ā*ḵ*
3sg. masc.	hū	-ō
3sg. fem.	hī	-ā
1pl.	*ᵃ*naḥnū	-ānū
2pl.masc.	'attem	-*ḵ*em
2pl. fem.	'atten	-*ḵ*en
3pl. masc.	hēmmā	-ām
3pl. fem.	hēnnāh	-ān

The unstressed forms are not independent words; they are always attached to another word, such as a verb, a preposition, or 'et. The set given here is used with 'et, which becomes 'ōt-; similar, but not identical, sets are used with verbs and as possessives (see Lesson 11).

To Be Remembered from Lesson 9

1 Any language can be expected to have 1st-, 2nd-, and 3rd-person pronouns, and most languages distinguish singular pronouns from plural pronouns.
2 Some languages have an extra 3rd-person pronoun to help distinguish between two 3rd-person entities in a discourse.
3 Other notions that can be expressed by pronouns vary from language to language. They include, but are not limited to, gender, politeness, and animacy.
4 If a language has case-marking, its pronouns will usually be case-marked.
5 Pronouns sometimes have unstressed forms that are different from the stressed forms.

10 | Reflexives and Passives

Languages need to express situations in which the subject does something to him- or herself. Many languages use REFLEXIVE pronouns to do that. A reflexive is a non-subject pronoun that refers to the same entity as the subject, typically in the same clause. Naturally the most important reflexives are the ones used as direct and indirect objects. The English system of reflexive pronouns is straightforward:

		subject	reflexive object
sg.	1	*I*	*myself*
	2	*you*	*yourself*
	3 masc.	*he*	*himself*
	3 fem.	*she*	*herself*
	3 neut.	*it*	*itself*
pl.	1	*we*	*ourselves*
	2	*you*	*yourselves*
	3	*they*	*themselves*

The plural -*selves* shows that *self* was originally a noun; the fact that the 1st- and 2nd-person forms begin with possessives (*my, your, our,* and in archaic English *thy*) points in the same direction, although it's surprising that the 3rd-person forms begin with the normal object forms of the non-reflexive pronouns. Note that whereas the 2sg. and 2pl. are mostly no longer distinguished in English, *yourself* is distinct from *yourselves*, basically because it can be.

The Mandarin system is even simpler: a single form *zìjǐ* 自己 'self' is used for all persons and numbers.

Navajo has a reflexive *'ádí-* which, like other object markers, always occurs on the verb, never as an independent pronoun. Like the Mandarin reflexive, it is used for all persons and numbers, e.g.:

> *Yiłdééh.* 'He's cleaning it off.'   *'Ádíldééh.* 'He's cleaning himself off.'
> *Yishdééh.* 'I'm cleaning it off.'   *'Ádíshdééh.* 'I'm cleaning myself off.'

If a reflexive object is used, the conjugation prefix *-ł-* must be changed to *-l-* (and zero-prefix must be changed to *-d-*); we will encounter that peculiarity again in the discussion of passive sentences below.

Spanish and Latin have a different system. In the 1st and 2nd persons (in Spanish, only the familiar 2nd person), there are no reflexive pronouns; you simply use the non-reflexive forms. After all, there can be no ambiguity. So in Spanish one says

> <u>Me</u> *miro en el espejo.*   'I'm looking at myself (*literally* me) in the mirror.'

and so also in Latin:

> *In speculō* <u>mē</u> *aspiciō.*

However, both Spanish and Latin have a 3rd-person reflexive pronoun – but only one, used for both numbers and all genders, and in Spanish also for the polite 2nd person. So if we put our *mirror* sentence into the 3sg. the result is:

> <u>Se</u> *mira en el espejo.* | *In speculō*   'He/she is looking at himself/herself in
> <u>sē</u> *aspicit.*   the mirror.'

and in the 3pl. the result is:

> <u>Se</u> *miran en el espejo.* | *In speculō*   'They're looking at themselves in
> <u>sē</u> *aspiciunt.*   the mirror.'

In Spanish we also find:

> *Usted se mira en el espejo.*   'You (polite) are looking at yourself
>   in the mirror.'
>
> *Ustedes se miran en el espejo.*   'You (pl. polite) are looking at yourselves
>   in the mirror.'

Of course Latin has a full set of caseforms for this pronoun (except that there is no nominative); they rhyme with the forms of the 2sg. pronoun.

Hebrew expresses reflexive direct objects very differently: there is a separate class of verbs that indicates reflexive objects. Reflexive verbs can be formed from basic verbs, e.g.:

bērēḵ 'he has blessed'   *hiṯbārēḵ* 'he has blessed himself'

hillēl 'he has praised'   *hiṯhallēl* 'he has boasted' ('praised himself')

heḥbī 'he has hidden (it)'   *hiṯḥabbē* 'he has hidden himself'

An intransitive basic verb automatically becomes transitive:

gāḏēl 'he has become great, he has   *hiṯgaddēl* 'he has made himself great'
  grown up'

qāḏēš 'he has become holy'   *hiṯqaddēš* 'he has made himself holy'

No reflexive pronoun is needed because the formation of the verb expresses the reflexive. This is unusual, but not unique: for instance, Algonkian languages also express reflexive direct objects by a special class of verbs.

When a reflexive that is not a direct object is needed, Hebrew usually uses the ordinary pronoun – not only for the 1st and 2nd persons, as in Spanish and Latin, but even for the 3rd person, e.g. in *Judges* 3:16:

> *wayya'aś*   *lō*   *'Ēhūḏ ḥereḇ*
> (and-make-IPF-3SGMASC for-him Ehud sword)
> 'and Ehud made (for) himself a sword'

That too is unusual, but not unique; for instance, Old English – i.e. English before the Norman Conquest – also used ordinary 3rd-person pronouns as reflexives (sometimes creating serious ambiguity).

Somewhat surprisingly, reflexive sentences are related to PASSIVE sentences in some languages, though not in others. The best way to understand passive sentences is to compare them with the corresponding ACTIVE sentences. Active is default – that is, active sentences are normally used – and in fact every example sentence you have seen so far is active. In the corresponding passives, the direct object of the active verb becomes the subject of the passive verb, e.g.:

> active: *The students read fifteen books*
> passive: *Fifteen books were read (by the students).*

The verbs have dotted underlining; as you can see, fifteen books is the direct object of the active sentence, but the subject of the passive sentence. Since the sentences say the same thing, it makes sense to ask why you would want to use a passive sentence instead of an active, especially since the active seems more straightforward and is often actually shorter. One possible reason is to emphasize the object of the active sentence by "promoting" it to subject. Another reason is that in a passive sentence the noun phrase that would have been the active subject – called the AGENT – can be omitted entirely, as the parentheses in the above example imply. The agent might not be relevant, or might already be known from context. But you can also use a passive sentence in order to be vague about the agent; for instance, you can say

> *Mistakes were made.*

without saying exactly who made them.

In English, passive verb phrases are always constructed from a form of the verb 'be' and a form of the main verb called the PAST PARTICIPLE; we will discuss the system in more detail in Lesson 14. In the rest of this lesson I will briefly describe how other languages construct passive verbs or verb phrases and how in some languages they overlap with reflexives.

Half the Latin system is like the English system: in the perfect tenses, a passive sentence is constructed with the perfect participle and a form of 'be'. The following active-passive pair is typical (the verbs are underlined):

> *Puer librum lēgit.*   'The boy read the book.'
> *Liber (ā puerō) lēctus est.* 'The book was read (by the boy).'

However, in the non-perfect tenses (which include the present and future) there are special passive verb forms. Here is the same pair of sentences in the present tense:

Puer librum legit.   'The boy is reading the book.'

Liber (ā puerō) legitur.   'The book is being read (by the boy).'

You can see that the passive form differs from the active form only by having a different ending.

Spanish, like the other descendants of Latin, has lost the special passive verb forms; it constructs all its passive sentences with 'be' and the past participle, like English. The four Latin sentences can be translated into Spanish as follows:

El niño leyó el libro.   'The boy read the book'

El libro fue leído (por el niño).   'The book was read (by the boy).'

El niño lee el libro.   'The boy is reading / reads the book.'

?*El libro es leído (por el niño).   'The book is read (by the boy).'

However, passive sentences are used much less often in Spanish than in English (or in Latin), and are mostly confined to written Spanish. The last passive sentence in the above list, in the present tense, is especially odd. You might conceivably use it as a stage direction for a play, but you definitely would not use it, even in writing, to describe a situation at the time of writing; you would use the active sentence instead.

But if passives are disfavored in Spanish – in fact almost completely avoided in natural speech – what do you do when you want to avoid mentioning who did something? A commonly used alternative is a 3rd-person reflexive sentence, which in Spanish can be interpreted as a passive. For instance, the sentence

Los frijoles se cuecen tres horas.

literally says 'The beans boil themselves (for) three hours.' But of course beans don't boil themselves; the sentence really means, 'The beans are boiled for three hours.' This is a standard substitute for passive sentences in many other Romance languages too, including French and Italian.

In Mandarin there is no special passive form of the verb, and there is no particle that converts a verb into a passive, but there is a passive construction. The agent is introduced by *bèi* 被 and precedes the verb (example from Yip and Rimmington 1997: 124):

Tā bèi lǎobǎn jiěgù le. 他被老板解雇了. 'He was dismissed by the boss.'
(he by boss   dismiss COMPLETIVE)

It is striking that passive sentences in Mandarin are identifiable by mention of an agent, whereas in European languages they are often used to avoid mentioning an agent. However, it is possible to construct an agentless passive in Mandarin simply by omitting the object of *bèi*, e.g.:

Tā bèi jiěgù le.   他被解雇了.   'He got fired.'

Mandarin, like Spanish, makes much less use of passives than English or Latin.

Just as Hebrew has a special type of derived verb to express reflexive direct objects, it has special derived passive verbs. The system is complex, as you can see from the following pairs of active and passive verbs:

šābar 'he has broken'	*nišbar* 'it has been broken'
śārap̄ 'he has burned (it)'	*niśrap̄* 'it has been burned'
šibbēr 'he has smashed'	*šubbar* 'it has been smashed'
biqqēš 'he has looked for (it/him)'	*buqqaš* 'he has been looked for'
higdīl 'he has made great'	*hogdal* 'he has been made great'
hišlīḵ 'he has thrown out'	*hušlaḵ* 'he has been thrown out'

The passive of basic verbs is marked by a prefixed *n-*; the passive of derived verbs (on which see Lesson 17) is marked by changing the vowels of the root-syllables, a process called ABLAUT.[1] As in the European languages we have looked at, the agent of a passive is introduced by a preposition in Hebrew, usually *lə-*, less often *min-* 'from'; but in most passive clauses the agent is unexpressed.

Unlike our other languages, Navajo cannot express the agent with a passive verb; passives are used only when the speaker does not wish to say who did something. In addition, for more conservative speakers, only 3rd-person non-human entities can be the subjects of passive verbs. A passive verb is recognizable by the fact that it has no object prefix in the position where one would appear in the active; in addition, the conjugation prefix immediately before the verb stem is sometimes altered, as in reflexives (see above). For instance:

---

[1] Some English verbs construct their past tenses and past participles by ablaut; a typical example is *sing*, past *sang*, past participle *sung*.

Mósí ch'ííłteeh. 'He's carrying the cat out.'
Mósí ch'élteeh. 'The cat is being carried out.'

In the active sentence the second *-í-* of the verb form is the direct object marker; in the passive sentence it is absent, and a (different) short vowel appears. In addition, the conjugation prefix *-ł-* of the active is replaced by *-l-* in the passive.

To express an English passive with a human subject, one must use a different construction in Navajo. The subject of the English passive is expressed by an *object* prefix, and there is an additional prefix expressing an *indefinite subject*. Thus a sentence like

Hastiin Nééz bi'dilzhééh. 'Mr. Long is being shaved.'

(Young and Morgan 1980, grammar p. 310)

literally means 'Mr. Long, someone (*-'di-*) is shaving him (*bi-*).' This is sometimes called an "agentive passive" (grammar, p. 310) because it shows the same replacement of conjugation prefixes as in passive verb forms; but we have already seen that reflexive forms also show the same peculiarity.

The constructions discussed in this lesson exhibit unusually great differences from language to language. In one sense that's an accident: every language is the result of a long (and mostly unrecorded) history in which all sorts of changes that were not inevitable happened for reasons that are usually not recoverable. But from another point of view it "makes sense" that languages vary so much in these particulars, because a language does not strictly need these complications. Speakers of Old English managed very well using ordinary pronouns to express reflexives; speakers of Spanish and Navajo use passives very seldom and can avoid them altogether without serious inconvenience.

Exercise

Consider the following English sentences:

Get up and wash yourself.
There's no time to lose – save yourselves!

Why are 2nd-person reflexive pronouns used in these sentences when there is no subject expressed? Why is the pronoun plural in the second sentence?

Convert the following English active sentences into passive sentences, putting the agent in parentheses:

The Romans destroyed Carthage.
The FBI is investigating the smugglers.
Farples will inevitably bloot the quarkle.

To Be Remembered from Lesson 10

1 A reflexive refers to an entity that is identical with the subject of the clause.
2 Some languages have special reflexive pronouns; others simply use the ordinary pronouns in reflexive function. A small minority of languages express reflexive direct objects with special verb forms.
3 In a passive sentence, the subject is what would be the object in the corresponding active sentence. The agent, which would be the subject in the corresponding active sentence, can be omitted; in some languages it is always omitted.
4 Many languages use passive sentences very sparingly; some substitute reflexive sentences for passives.

Further Reading

Quirk et al. 1980 deal with English reflexive pronouns on pp. 211–13 and have a very detailed discussion of English passive clauses on pp. 801–11. Butt and Benjamin 2011: 391–407 is an equally detailed discussion of Spanish passives and alternatives to them. Pinkster 2015, ch. 5 discusses Latin passives and reflexives in depth.

11 | Possession

One of the important things a language has to convey is what belongs to whom. Our sample languages do that in several different ways, but all of them build complex noun phrases: the possessor is part of the noun phrase headed by the thing possessed.

Mandarin has the simplest and most transparent system. Usually the possessor is followed by the PARTICLE *de*,[1] which in turn is followed by the thing possessed; that holds whether the possessor is a full noun phrase or just a pronoun (although in the latter case the particle is usually run together with the pronoun when Mandarin is written in Roman letters):

wǒde shū	我的书	'my book'
Xiǎogāo de shū	小高的书	'Xiaogao's book'
Xībānyá de wáng de jiàochē	西班牙的王的轿车	'the King of Spain's limousine'

(Spain -'s king -'s limousine)

The only exception is that when the possessor is a pronoun and the possessed noun indicates a family member, *de* is very often omitted; we have already encountered *wǒ yéye* 'my grandfather', for instance.

---

[1] A particle is a small word, often unstressed, that performs a grammatical function.

In our other sample languages it makes a difference whether the possessor is a personal pronoun; we will deal with pronominal possessors at the end of this lesson.

For possessors that are full noun phrases Spanish has a simple system: the possessor is introduced by the preposition *de*, and the prepositional phrase follows the thing possessed:

la hermana de Lucía	'Lucy's sister'
el rey de España	'the King of Spain'
la limusina del rey de España	'the King of Spain's limousine' (del = de el)

The fact that the Spanish preposition and the Mandarin particle resemble one another is a sheer accident, but the difference in the order of possessor and possessed is not. A phrase like *the King of Spain's limousine* is a noun phrase, and, as a general rule, in complex noun phrases the items modifying the head noun precede it in Mandarin, whereas in Spanish they follow it if they are stressed, only a few unstressed items preceding it. Here are the two translations of that noun phrase with the head noun 'limousine' underlined:

Xībānyá de wáng de jiàochē
la limusina del rey de España

In the Mandarin noun phrase the head is phrase-final; in the Spanish noun phrase it is phrase-initial, preceded only by the unstressed article *la*. (Articles will be discussed in Lesson 23.)

Latin has an equally simple but completely different system: the possessor is in the GENITIVE case. For instance (genitive endings underlined):

Caesaris librī	'Caesar's books'
domus amīcī nostrī	'the house of our friend Marcus' (all three
Mārcī	items in the genitive because 'our friend Marcus'
	is the possessing noun phrase)

In Latin the possessor can either precede or follow the thing possessed, although if it is short it tends to precede.

Hebrew has yet another way of indicating that the referent of one noun possesses the referent of another. Basically the nouns are simply juxtaposed in the order possessed + possessor; but the first of the two nouns appears in an abbreviated form called the CONSTRUCT STATE, and a noun in the construct state cannot be preceded by the definite article *ha-* 'the' even though it is definite in meaning. For instance, here are the usual forms of 'word', without and with the definite article:

dābār 'word'   *haddābār* 'the word'
dəbārīm 'words'   *haddəbārīm* 'the words'

But in the construct state we find instead:

dəbar ᵉlōhīm 'the word of God'
dibrē hammelek 'the words of the king'

There are rules for forming the construct state of nouns of particular shapes, but that detail is still a significant complication of Hebrew grammar; thus the syntax is very simple, but it is accompanied by fairly complex inflection. Construct states are typical of Semitic languages and occur in some other Afroasiatic[2] languages, but outside that family they are rare.

English has *two* ways of indicating possession by full noun phrases, and that is very unusual. One is a particle spelled *-'s* (or just *-'*, if it is attached to a plural noun already ending in the plural marker *-(e)s*). Except for the fact that it is not used with pronouns, it is very much like Mandarin *de:*

Lucy's sister
Rupert's book
the King of Spain's limousine

Note that, like *de*, it can be attached to an entire complex noun phrase, in the last case *the King of Spain* (it's not *Spain's* limousine, it's *the King of Spain's*). It can even be attached to a noun phrase that contains an entire clause, e.g.

[*the other guy whose name I don't know*]*'s shoes.*

As with Mandarin *de*, a possessor to which this particle is attached precedes the thing possessed.

The other English possessive construction uses the preposition *of* and is exactly parallel to the Spanish construction with the preposition *de*. For instance,

the center of the city

---

[2] The larger family to which the Semitic (sub)family belongs.

translates into Spanish word for word as

el centro de la ciudad

This type of possessive follows the thing possessed, because any prepositional phrase inside a noun phrase follows the head noun. After all, we also say

the man with the yellow hat,
not **the with the yellow hat man.*

The two English constructions often mean the same thing (although *of* has a broader range of meaning – see below); but even when they do, they're not always interchangeable. While *Lucy's sister* is native English, *the sister of Lucy* is not; it sounds like something a foreigner might say. Conversely, *the center of the city* is more natural than *the city's center* in most contexts. On the other hand, *the King of Spain's limousine* is not clearly better or worse than *the limousine of the King of Spain*, although the latter sounds a little more formal or less colloquial.

Navajo indicates possession in a different way, which we will not be able to discuss until we have discussed possession by pronouns; I therefore postpone it until the end of this lesson.

Note that Mandarin *de*, Spanish *de*, English *of*, the Latin genitive case, and the Hebrew possessive construction are used for a wide range of relationships that can be thought of as "belonging" but aren't literal cases of possession. For instance, the following are completely normal, and so are their English translations:

Zhōngguǒ de cānguǎn 中国的餐馆 'the restaurants of China'

(Ho 2002: 1)

las ciudades de la frontera 'the cities of the frontier'
propter lātitūdinem fossae mūrīque altitūdinem 'because of the width of the ditch and the height of the wall'

(Caesar, Gallic War II.12.2)

mayim hayYardēn 'the water of the Jordan'

This is another way in which Hebrew compensates for its relative lack of adjectives. For instance,

diḇrē ᵉmeṯ 'words of truth'

is the normal way of saying 'true words' or 'a true discourse'. The range of usage of the English particle -'s is significantly narrower; it tends to be used to express literal possession, although it can occasionally express other relationships.

When the possessor is a personal pronoun, English and Spanish express the relationship by a possessive adjective corresponding to the pronoun; Latin does the same for the 1st- and 2nd-person pronouns. Both English and Spanish have two sets of forms depending on the context in which the possessive adjective occurs: there is a fuller form used when the possessive adjective is a complement of a linking verb (called PREDICATIVE position; see Lesson 8) and a less full form used when the possessive adjective is inside a noun phrase (called ATTRIBUTIVE position). The systems can be tabulated as follows:

	English		Spanish		Latin
	attributive	predicative	attributive	predicative	
1sg.	*my*	*mine*	*mi*	*mío*	*meus*
2sg. familiar	*your*	*yours*[3]	*tu*	*tuyo*	*tuus*
2sg. polite	(*your*	*yours*)	*su*	*suyo*	(*tuus*)
3sg. masc.	*his*	*his*	*su*	*suyo*	
3sg. fem.	*her*	*hers*	*su*	*suyo*	
3sg. neut.	*its*	—			
1pl.	*our*	*ours*	*nuestro*	*nuestro*	*noster*
2pl. familiar	*your*	*yours*	*vuestro*	*vuestro*	*vester*
2pl. polite	(*your*	*yours*)	*su*	*suyo*	(*vester*)
3pl.	*their*	*theirs*	*su*	*suyo*	

The Spanish syncretism of all 3rd-person and polite 2nd-person forms is very striking. Context disambiguates, for example:

> *Ponga su documento sobre la mesa, por favor.* 'Please put your paper on the table.' (polite command, subjunctive singular; therefore *su* must be polite 2sg.)
> *Pusieron su documento en la caja.* 'They put their paper in the box.' (3pl. verb, not a command; therefore *su* is 3pl.)

The Latin possessive adjectives each have forms for all three genders, both numbers, and all five cases, like all other adjectives do. The Spanish

---

[3] Formerly *thy* and *thine*, parallel to *my* and *mine*; see Lesson 9.

possessive adjectives have plurals in -s, and those that end in -o in the masculine singular have plurals in -os, feminines in -a, and feminine plurals in -as, like all other adjectives. Those complications are not noted in the table above.

The difference between attributive and predicative forms can be illustrated with a pair of English and Spanish examples:

> *This is my book.*   *This book is mine.*
> *Este es mi libro.*   *Este libro es mío.*

Apparently there is no predicative form of English *its*; at least, all attempts to construct example sentences with it sound very odd to me.

Unlike English and Spanish, Latin uses the genitive caseforms of the 3rd-person pronoun to express 'his, her, its, their' (see Lesson 9). Since they are not adjectives, they do not have multiple forms for gender, number, and case. Compare the following phrases, the first set with the possessive adjective 'our', the second with *eius* 'his/her/its':

> *liber noster* 'our book, nuestro libro'
> *librī nostrī* 'our books, nuestros libros'
> *mēnsa nostra* 'our table, nuestra mesa'
> *mēnsae nostrae* 'our tables, nuestras mesas'

but

> *liber eius* 'his/her book, su libro'
> *librī eius* 'his/her books, sus libros'
> *mēnsa eius* 'his/her table, su mesa'
> *mēnsae eius* 'his/her tables, sus mesas'

It might have occurred to you to ask: if Latin doesn't use the genitive caseforms of the 1st- and 2nd-person pronouns (see Lesson 9) to express possession, what does it use them for? It turns out that there are a few other things that the genitive is used to express.[4] For instance, 'which of us' is expressed as *quis nostrum*, with a genitive of *nōs* 'we, us', and 'longing for you' is *dēsīderium tuī*, literally 'desire of you'. The verb *meminisse* 'to remember' exceptionally governs

---

[4] I am grateful to an anonymous reviewer for reminding me of some of these.

an object in the genitive, so 'remember me' is *mementō meī*. (This last peculiarity is so unusual that I won't be mentioning it again.)

In Hebrew and Navajo a pronoun that is a possessor is AFFIXED (attached) to the noun that it possesses. In Hebrew the affixes are suffixes, following the noun; in Navajo they are prefixes, preceding the noun. In both languages they are obviously similar to the personal pronouns (in Hebrew they are similar to, though not identical with, the unstressed pronoun suffixes used with verbs and prepositions). Thus with the noun 'horse':

	Hebrew	Navajo	
1sg.	*sūsī*	*shilíí'*	'my horse'
2sg. masc.	*sūsəkā*	*nilíí'*	'your (m.) horse'
2sg. fem.	*sūsēk*	"	'your (f.) horse'
3sg. masc.	*sūsō*	*bilíí'*	'his horse'
3sg. fem.	*sūsāh*	"	'her horse'
1pl.	*sūsēnū*	*nihilíí'*	'our horse'
2pl. masc.	*sūsəkem*	"	'your (pl. m.) horse'
2pl. fem.	*sūsəken*	"	'your (pl. f.) horse'
3pl. masc.	*sūsām*	*bilíí'*	'their (m.) horse'
3pl. fem.	*sūsān*	"	'their (f.) horse'

(In Navajo the initial *ł-* of *łíí'* 'horse' is voiced to *-l-* after a prefix by a phonological rule.) In its possessive affixes each language makes all and only the distinctions that it does for its independent pronouns: Hebrew marks the gender of the possessor in all the 2nd- and 3rd-person forms, while Navajo never marks gender at all; Hebrew consistently distinguishes between singular and plural possessors, while Navajo does so only for the 1st and 2nd persons, and in addition Navajo has only a single form for 1pl. and 2pl. On the other hand, all the plural possessors in Navajo can be prefixed with *da-* 'each', and corresponding to the animate 3rd-person pronoun *hó* there is a possessive prefix *ha-* or *ho-* (not included in the table above). Finally, Navajo has an alternative 3rd-person prefix *yi-*, which is used instead of *bi-* to distinguish between two 3rd-person entities in the discourse. The rules governing the use of the two prefixes are complex (see Young and Morgan 1980, grammar p. 25), but the following example (taken from Young and Morgan's discussion) gives some idea how the system works.

> *Shimá   shizhé'é   nádzáago   yi'éé'   yich'į'   ch'éyiiz'ah.*
> (my-mother my-father has-returned-when his-clothes him-toward
>   has-serially-tossed-them-out-as-flat-flexible-objects)[5]
> 'When my father returned, my mother tossed his clothes out to him.'

If the speaker had said *bi'éé'*, it would have meant that she tossed *her* clothes out to him.

Unlike our other sample languages, Navajo uses the pronominal prefixes *together with* a full noun phrase to express possession by that noun phrase. For example (the possessive markers are underlined):

M   *nǔhái de mǎ*   女孩的马
    (girl   -'s horse)

E   *the girl's horse*

S   *el   caballo   de la   niña*
    (the horse   of the   girl)

L   *puellae equus*

H   *sūs   hā'almā*
    (horse   the-youngwoman)

N   *ch'ikę́ę́h   bilį́į́'*
    (youngwoman her-horse)

There is no other way of expressing this relation in Navajo.

There is also a further complication involving Navajo possessives: some nouns cannot be used without a possessive prefix. Thus you can say *shimá* 'my mother', *nimá* 'your (sg.) mother', etc., but you can't just say 'mother'; you have to say *'amá* 'someone's mother', using a prefix for indefinite possessor. Most of the nouns in question are INALIENABLY possessed – that is, you can't give them away. The obvious examples are kinship terms and body-part terms. I can "give you my hand" in any number of ways, but it will still be identifiable as "my hand" even if I cut it off. So also my mother: she remains my mother even though she is long deceased.

---

[5]   Navajo verbs that reference handling objects describe the shape or classification of the objects in question (see the following lesson); what is done with the objects is expressed by the prefixes on the verb.

It might have occurred to you that the reflexive pronouns mentioned in the last lesson have possessive forms too, translating English 'my own', 'your own', etc. They do, and it won't surprise you to learn that each of our sample languages handles that detail somewhat differently. We don't need to discuss reflexive possessives here; your instructor will show you how the language most of interest to you expresses that relation.

Even apart from that, this survey does not exhaust the ways that languages express possession. For instance, many languages, including some of the ones discussed here, also have verbs meaning 'have', 'possess', and/or 'belong to'. In Latin you can use the dative case with the verb 'be' to say that the subject of 'be' belongs to the noun phrase in the dative, e.g.

> *Nōmen mihi Mārcō   est.* 'My name is Marcus.'
> (name to-me (to-)Marcus is)[6]

In Hebrew, which has no verb meaning 'have', the normal way of saying 'X has Y' is 'there is Y to X', e.g.

> *Yēš   lī   bēn.* 'I have a son.'
> ('there-is to-me son')

You've already figured out that the fit between meaning and its expression in human language is not one-to-one but many-to-many, but even if you hadn't realized that, a good look at how languages express possession would convince you.

Exercise

The language exemplified here uses a mixed system to indicate possession, number, and case. Here is a small part of its system; describe it as accurately as you can.

---

[6] The name 'Marcus' is put in the dative too because it refers to the same person as 'me', which has to be in the dative.

talo 'house' talot 'houses'

talon katto 'the house's roof' talojen katot 'the houses' roofs'

talossa 'in the house' taloissa 'in the houses'

talosta 'out of the house' taloista 'out of the houses'

taloni 'my house' taloni 'my houses'

talosi 'your (sg.) house' talosi 'your (sg.) houses'

talossani 'in my house' taloissani 'in my houses'

talostani 'out of my house' taloistani 'out of my houses'

To Be Remembered from Lesson 11

Our six languages mark possession by full noun phrases in five different ways: case-marking (Latin), adpositions (English and Spanish), phrasal particles (English and Mandarin), the construct state (Hebrew), and affixes on the possessed noun (Navajo). They mark possession by pronouns in three different ways: possessive adjectives (the European languages), affixes (Hebrew and Navajo), and a phrasal particle (Mandarin). They differ far more in this respect than they do in marking the verb and its noun phrases (subject, objects, etc.) – because they can: whereas the larger structure of clauses is universal, possession is a "local" detail of noun phrases and can vary more from language to language without disrupting the larger clause structure.

12 | Gender, Concord, and Noun Classifications

In the pronoun systems of European languages we found that 3rd-person forms are marked for gender. (In Spanish so are some other pronouns; see Lesson 9 for discussion.) English has a "natural" system of gender, corresponding to real-world gender distinctions. In both Spanish and Latin, however, the genders are really CONCORD CLASSES. We will first describe the Latin system, then discuss the (very modest) ways in which the Spanish system differs from it.

Every noun in Latin is assigned to one of the three gender classes, masculine, feminine, and neuter; its gender is part of the grammatical identity of the noun. To a very limited extent the system is natural: male persons and animals are usually indicated by masculine nouns, and female persons and animals are usually indicated by feminine nouns. Otherwise, however, the assignment of nouns to genders is largely arbitrary. The following are typical:

masculine	feminine	neuter
pater 'father'	*māter* 'mother'	*nōmen* 'name'
oculus 'eye'	*auris* 'ear'	*ōs* 'mouth'
pēs 'foot'	*manus* 'hand'	*caput* 'head'
mōns 'mountain'	*terra* 'earth, land'	*mare* 'sea'
animus 'spirit, mind'	*mēns* 'mind, attitude'	*cor* 'heart'

In spite of its complexity and arbitrariness this classification is useful, because it is the basis of the CONCORD system. Within a noun phrase, an adjective that modifies the head noun must agree with it in gender; so must demonstratives like 'this' and 'that'; so must any 3rd-person pronoun that refers back to the noun; in addition, an adjective that is a complement after a linking verb must agree in gender with its subject. Here are some examples of gender concord in Latin, with the concord markers underlined:

pater meus 'my father'   *māter mea* 'my mother'   *nōmen meum* 'my name'
hic oculus 'this eye'   *haec auris* 'this ear'   *hoc ōs* 'this mouth'
Pēs laesus est: est vulnus in eō. '(My) foot is injured: there's a wound on it.'
Manus laesa est: est vulnus in eā. '(My) hand is injured: there's a wound on it.'

The requirement that 3rd-person pronouns must agree in gender with their ANTECEDENTS (the nouns they refer back to) makes it easier to keep track of multiple inanimate objects in a discourse, but there is another advantage to this concord system too. As we saw in Lesson 6, the case-marking system of Latin makes much greater flexibility of word order possible. So does the concord system; adjectives and demonstratives can be shifted around and separated from their nouns with no loss of clarity. Latin word order still isn't exactly "free," but you have a lot more options than in any of our other sample languages.

The Spanish system is somewhat simpler than the Latin system. For one thing, there is no neuter gender; each noun is either masculine or feminine. Latin neuter nouns that survive in Spanish (its direct descendant) have been shifted into either the masculine or the feminine class, or occasionally into both; for instance, *nombre* 'name' is masculine, while *mar* 'sea' is usually masculine but is feminine when used metaphorically, in poetry, and in technical or professional discourse relating to the sea. (Latin *caput* and *cor* have been replaced by derivatives *cabeza* (fem.) and *corazón* (masc.); *ōs* has been replaced by *boca* (fem.), a completely different word.) Moreover, the gender of large numbers of Spanish nouns is predictable from their shape: nouns in *-o* are masculine, except for *mano* 'hand' and a few others, and a large majority of nouns in *-a* are feminine. (The Latin distribution of genders is much more complex, with many more exceptions.) The only new complication is that there are a few gender mismatches in Spanish; for instance *la persona* 'the person' is feminine regardless of who it refers to.

The Hebrew system of gender functions almost exactly like the Spanish system, but is less transparent. The default class is masculine. Nouns denoting females are feminine, regardless of their shape. So are derived nouns in -*ā*, many of which are transparently derived from masculine nouns or verb roots, e.g.:

meleḵ 'king'	:	*malkā* 'queen', *mamlāḵā* 'kingdom'
nilḥam 'he has fought'	:	*milḥāmā* 'battle'

There are also a few fossilized feminine derivatives in -*ṯ*, e.g. *deleṯ* 'door', *daʿaṯ* 'knowledge'. Body parts that occur in pairs are normally feminine, e.g. *ʿayin* 'eye','*ōzen* 'ear', *yāḏ* 'hand', *regel* 'foot'; so are nouns denoting inhabitable places, e.g. *ʾereṣ* 'land', *ʿīr* 'city'. But in addition there are feminine nouns whose gender cannot be deduced from their meaning or shape, e.g. *ʾeḇen* 'stone', *ʾēš* 'fire', *ḥereḇ* 'sword', *nep̄eš* 'life'.

Such partially arbitrary systems of concord classes are not evenly distributed among the world's languages – for instance, they are very common in Europe but fairly rare among the native languages of North America – but hundreds of languages have them. Small systems are common; the commonest are masculine vs. feminine (as in Semitic and many European languages) and animate vs. inanimate (as in Algonkian and some European languages). But larger systems are not rare, including some with so many classes that they are not usually called "genders." Perhaps the best known are the noun class systems of the Niger-Congo languages, including the Bantu subgroup; for instance, even Swahili, a somewhat simplified Bantu language, has more than half a dozen concord classes, and some languages have many more.

Mandarin has no gender – but it has a roughly comparable system of CLASSIFIERS, sometimes called "measure words." When a noun is preceded in its noun phrase by a numeral (or other quantifying word, like *bàn* 半 'half' or *jǐ* 几 'several'), or by a demonstrative (*zhèi* 这 'this' or *nà, nèi* 那 'that'), an appropriate classifier must be placed immediately before the noun. The classifier is chosen according to the meaning of the noun. The system is very large and complex, with a number of unexpected quirks. The following examples of noun phrases using *sān* 三 'three' are typical (see also Yip and Rimmington 1997: 15–19):

sān ge rén 三个人	'three people'	(*gè*, classifier for people, usually destressed)
sān zhī niǎo 三只鸟	'three birds'	(*zhī*, default classifier for animals)
sān pǐ mǎ 三匹马	'three horses'	(*pǐ*, classifier for horses)

sān tiáo shé 三条蛇	'three snakes'	(*tiáo*, classifier for long flexible things)
sān kē xīng 三颗星	'three stars'	(*kē*, classifier for small round objects)
sān lì shā 三粒砂	'three grains of sand'	(*lì*, classifier for tiny roundish objects)
sān liàng qìchē 三辆汽车	'three cars'	(*liàng*, classifier for vehicles)
sān jià fēijī 三架飞机	'three planes'	(*jià*, classifier for airplanes)
sān bǎ dāo 三把刀	'three knives'	(*bǎ*, classifier for things that can be handled)

This is just a sample; there are more than a dozen other classifiers in common use for large classes of nouns, and many more for very specific classes (flowers, hats, songs, etc.). In addition, nouns denoting containers and standard measures are used as classifiers, as are names of collections and parts, e.g.:

sān bēi chá 三杯茶	'three cups of tea'	(*bēi* 'cup, glass')
sān mǎ bù 三码布	'three yards of cloth'	(*mǎ* 'yard')
sān tào kèběn 三套课本	'three sets of textbooks'	(*tào* 'set')
sān dī shuǐ 三滴水	'three drops of water'	(*dī* 'drop')

That part of the system is very like English. Finally, there are classifiers for small but indefinite numbers and quantities:

| *yi xiē shū* 一些书 | 'a few books, some books' |
| *yi diǎnr shuǐ* 一点儿水 | 'a little water' |

That, too, resembles English usage.

The full Mandarin classifier system is much harder to learn than a typical gender system, even though it is based on the meanings of the nouns, partly because of its sheer size and complexity and partly because the shape of a noun gives you no clue to what its classifier should be. Not surprisingly, there is an optional simplification of the system: all the classifiers for specific nouns, like the ones listed in the first block above, can be replaced with *gè*, the classifier for people! Of course if you do that you are more or less declaring, "I am not a native speaker," even though you're speaking grammatical Mandarin; but that is not necessarily a problem in China. (See the excursus to this lesson.)

To a limited extent the Mandarin classifier system has some of the same advantages as a concord system; for instance, if there is a noun already in the discourse context, you can omit it in some cases without creating ambiguity. For instance, if you've been talking with the sales clerk about buying a notebook and a pen, and you finally make up your mind and say

Wǒ gèng xǐhuān zhèi běn.   我更喜欢这本.   'I prefer this one.'
(I   more like   this CLASSIFIER)

the clerk knows that you're talking about a notebook, because *běn* is the classifier for books.

Classifier systems are especially common among eastern Asian and Oceanic languages, but they are also found in Mesoamerica (e.g. in the Mayan languages), in some Native American languages spoken along the northwest coast of North America, and in West Africa.

Navajo and the other Athabaskan languages have a similar classification system, but it appears in a different place in the grammar: in sentences describing the position or motion of an object, or the handling of an object by a human being, *the verb denotes the shape of the object*, while what happens to it or is done with it is expressed by adverbial prefixes, postpositional phrases, etc. So far as I can discover, no other family of languages has a similar system. Thus 'give' is expressed by different verbs in Navajo depending on what gets given, e.g.:

Naaltsoos shaa ní'aah	'Give me the book.'	(-*'aah* 'handle a compact object')
Sis shaa nílé.	'Give me the belt.'	(-*lé* 'handle a long flexible object')
Tsin shaa nítįįh.	'Give me the pole.'	(-*tįįh* 'handle a long rigid object')
Beeldléí shaa níltsóós.'	'Give me the blanket.'	(-*tsóós* 'handle a flat flexible object')
Tó shaa níkaad.	'Give me (a cup of) water.'	(-*kaad* 'handle a container with its contents')
'Eii shaa nínííł.	'Give me those.'	('*eii* 'that', -*nííł* 'handle several')

There are nearly twenty sets of these classificatory verbs, some including four separate verbs (for handling, throwing, unimpeded motion of the object, and position of the object), and learning how they classify nouns is comparable to learning the Mandarin system of classifiers.

Excursus

Mandarin is both the official national language of China and the majority language in that country; it is spoken by more than 960 million people. Other Chinese languages are:

Wú, spoken by more than 80 million people in the area of Shànghǎi;

Gàn, spoken by more than 20 million people in Jiāngxī and neighboring provinces;

Xiāng, spoken by almost 40 million people in and around Húnán province;

Mǐn, the dialects of Fújiàn province and Táiwān – possibly at least four mutually unintelligible languages;

Hākká (Yuè name; Mandarin Kèjiāhuà), spoken by about 30 million people throughout southern China;

Yuè, also called Cantonese, spoken by about 60 million people in and around Guǎngdōng province and very widely overseas.

Some recent work recognizes three additional languages spoken by (relatively) small populations. The diversity of Chinese has been compared to that of Romance languages. Because everyone must learn Mandarin there are millions of non-native speakers of that language who are nevertheless Hàn (ethnic Chinese).

Exercise

Here are some noun phrases in an unfamiliar language that has concord classes. What is unusual about how this concord system works?

	singular	plural
'great king'	*orotstse walo*	*orocci lāñc*
'great queen'	*orotstsa lāntsa*	*orotstsana lantsona*
'large fire'	*orotstse puwar*	*orotstsana pwāra*
'good father'	*kartse pācer*	*kreñc pacera*
'good mother'	*kartsa mācer*	*krenta macera*
'good name'	*kartse ñem*	*krenta ñemna*

To Be Remembered from Lesson 12

1 Grammatical "gender" is really a system of concord that helps the language user keep track of what goes with what in a clause or discourse. Genders are concord classes of nouns.
2 Concord classes are widespread but unevenly distributed among the world's languages; small systems are commonest, but very large systems also exist.
3 Classifier systems are also widespread among the world's languages.

Further Reading

Corbett 1991 is an excellent exploration of concord classes among the world's languages, with detailed discussion of numerous interesting cases.

13 Case Systems and Adpositions: The Latin System

As we have already seen, the Latin case system performs several different syntactic and semantic functions. If we list the Latin cases with their principal functions, you can see how diverse they are:

case	functions
nominative	(1) subject of a finite verb; (2) complement
accusative	(1) direct object; (2) object of most prepositions; (3) extent of time or space; (4) subject of an infinitive
genitive	(1) possession; (2) other relations translatable by *of*, especially partitive; (3) complement of some adjectives
dative	(1) indirect object; (2) purpose
ablative	(1) instrument; (2) object of some prepositions; (3) time at which; (4) degree of difference; (5) standard of comparison; (6) complement of some adjectives; (7) absolute constructions (an equivalent of subordinate clauses)

We have already seen examples of some of these. We don't need to discuss all the rest, but it might be good to illustrate a few.

- prepositions
  - with the accusative:

     in oppidum 'into the town'

     ad oppidum 'at the town; to the town'

     contrā opīniōnem 'against expectations'

  – with the ablative:

     in oppidō 'in the town'

     cum mīlitibus '(together) with the soldiers'

     magnō cum dolōre 'with great sorrow'

- expressions of time
  - with the accusative:

     trēs diēs 'for three days'

  – with the ablative:

     tertiā diē 'on the third day'

- other uses of the ablative:

     Arborem <u>dolābrā</u> caesit. 'He cut down the tree <u>with an ax</u>.'

     <u>Litterīs acceptīs</u> in Ītaliam quam prīmum profectus est. '<u>The letter being received</u>, he set out for Italy as soon as possible.'

This is an extraordinary grab-bag of functions. Some are purely syntactic (e.g. subjects and objects); others are purely semantic (i.e. they express meaning directly, e.g. in expressions of time and space); a few are somewhat difficult to classify. However, they all can be described in a single phrase: *they specify the relations of noun phrases to the rest of the sentence.* That is what case systems are for.

Latin does not have nearly enough distinct cases to specify all the relations of noun phrases – not even considering that subject-and-object relations are not likely to be confused with specifications of time and space (for example). Most (all?) case-marking languages don't have enough cases for that (although Finnish, with fifteen cases, comes a lot closer to doing so, and there are Northeast Caucasian languages that can attach several case markers to a single noun, yielding very specific meanings). So Latin and other case-marking languages typically use adpositions to specify the relations of noun phrases more closely.

That raises an obvious question: if you have to use adpositions anyway, and if there is a default word order for subjects and objects, why not use only word order and adpositions to mark the relations of noun phrases? That is almost the solution that Spanish, a direct ancestor of Latin, has evolved: except for the personal pronouns, noun phrase relations are marked entirely by word order and prepositions (see Lessons 3, 6, and 7). The same can be said of English, except that in English we also have the particle -'s; Hebrew and Navajo use only word order, particles, and adpositions in the same functions; in some circumstances Mandarin also uses multiple verbs. For instance, let's translate one of the Latin sentences above into our other five languages, giving word-for-word glosses of each with the inflectional markers in small caps:

L   *Arborem <u>dolābrā</u> caesit.*
      (tree-ACC ax-ABL   chop-PERF-3SG)

S   *Cortó   el   árbol <u>con</u> <u>hacha</u>.*
      (cut-PRET-3SG the-MASC tree   with ax)

E   *He cut down the tree <u>with an ax</u>.*

H   *Kāra<u>t</u>   'e<u>t</u>-   hā'ē<u>ṣ</u>   <u>bəgarzen</u>.*
      (cut-PERF-3SGMASC   PTCL   the-tree with-ax)

N   *Tsin <u>tsénił bee</u>   yítséél.*
      (tree ax   3SG-with 3SG-PERF-chop)[1]

M   *<u>Yòng fǔ</u> kǎn le   shù.*
      (use   ax fell COMPLETIVE tree)

This raises a general point about inflection. Since a language can do without any, all inflection is a real complication of the grammar. There are other ways to complicate the grammar – consider the Mandarin classifier system discussed in the preceding lesson – but a language with lots of inflection can't be maximally simple. It also can't be maximally straightforward. The artificial languages that mathematicians and logicians have devised never have anything like inflection in them, because they're more consistent and straightforward without it.

I'm bringing this up because someone might have suggested to you that Latin is somehow more logical, or more perfect, or in some way superior to languages like English. I can assure you from almost fifty years of experience with Latin that that's just not true. People who say that kind of thing are making a *cultural* judgment that has nothing to do with a language's structure; in fact, almost any value judgment about a language turns out to be cultural or social rather than structural. Don't ever suppose that one language is superior to another internally, because of its structure! That's never true, and you really don't want to make such an elementary blunder.

---

[1] The 3sg. subject is unmarked.

Exercise

Give an informal description of the case system of this language in your own words. You need to bear the following phonological rules in mind:

the nasal *n* is replaced by *m̩* at the end of a word and before *ś*

s is replaced by *ts* immediately following a nasal

nasals can be dropped before consonant clusters that begin with nasals, such as *mp* and *m̩ts.*

Kantwo koynane mäsketär. 'The tongue is located in the mouth.'

Lwāntse kantwa lkāskau. 'I see the animal's tongue.'

käntwāntse āke 'the tip of the tongue'

Kantwasa yokäm̩. 'It drinks with its tongue.'

kantwaśc 'to the tongue'

kantwamem̩ 'from the tongue'

kantwane 'in / on the tongue'

kantwampa 'together with the tongue'

Cey käntwāñ pärkari skentär. 'Those tongues are long.'

Lwāsam̩ts käntwām̩ lkāskau. 'I see the animals' tongues.'

käntwām̩ts akenta 'the tips of the tongues'

Käntwāntsa yokäm̩. 'They drink with their tongues.'

käntwām̩śc 'to the tongues'

käntwānmem̩ 'from the tongues'

käntwānne 'in / on the tongues'

käntwāmpa 'together with the tongues'

To Be Remembered from Lesson 13

Case systems are fairly widespread among the world's languages. They perform the same grammatical functions as word order (of subjects and objects) and adpositions, often together with those other devices; they are therefore not necessary, although (like any grammatical device) they open up additional expressive possibilities for a language.

Further Reading

Blake 2001 is a good exploration of case-marking systems.

14 | Tense, Aspect, and Auxiliary Verbs: The English Verb System

The verb systems of languages differ at least as much as any other part of their grammars, simply because the number of things a verb form can express simultaneously is very large and their inflection therefore *can* be very complex (although it need not be). We will therefore discuss the verb systems of our sample languages individually, taking each description as the starting-point for the next.

First we need to define a couple of terms. The TENSE of a verb form expresses the *time* at which the action of the verb takes place; it can also express the relation of that time to other points in time. The ASPECT of a verb form expresses the internal structure of the verb's action; it can also signify that the speaker isn't interested in the action's internal structure (see further below), and various ideas related to the structure of actions. The English verb system is structured around the concept of tense; aspect is expressed much less consistently.

English has three simple tenses, usually called PRESENT, PAST, and FUTURE. The present indicates that the action of the verb is going on at the time of speaking; the past indicates that it occurred prior to the time of speaking; while the future indicates that the speaker expects it to happen at some subsequent time. For instance:

Now I see the bridge. (present)

When we turned the corner I <u>saw</u> the bridge. (past)

You <u>will see</u> the bridge shortly before we get there. (future)

Note that while the present and past are constructed from the ROOT of the verb (the basic part that indicates the verb's meaning), the future is constructed with an AUXILIARY VERB *will* followed by the bare verb root.

English also has three ANTERIOR tenses, traditionally called "PERFECT" tenses, which indicate that the action of the verb occurred before some specified point in time. The anterior tenses are constructed with the relevant tenses of the auxiliary verb *have* plus a form of the main verb called the PAST PARTICIPLE:

I <u>have seen</u> the Golden Gate Bridge. (present perfect)

They <u>had seen</u> the bridge from some distance away but couldn't figure out how to get to it. (past perfect, or pluperfect)

By the time you've been in Venice a day or two you <u>will have seen</u> dozens of bridges. (future perfect)

As you can see, the future perfect indicates that the action will occur before some specified time in the future; the past perfect, or "pluperfect," indicates that the action occurred before some specified time in the past; and the present perfect indicates that the action occurred before the time of speaking. That ought to mean that the present perfect is equivalent to the simple past, but there is actually a subtle difference in meaning: the present perfect implies that the action of the verb is still somehow relevant at the time of speaking, whereas the simple past doesn't imply anything about the action's relevance. For instance, the first example implies that the action of seeing the Golden Gate Bridge is still relevant, because it's a famous sight that you either have or haven't seen. Moreover, if you say[1]

I have taken my mother to see the Golden Gate Bridge. She died a few years ago.

there is something odd about the discourse, since the fact that your mother is no longer alive renders the first sentence less relevant to the situation at the time of speaking.

Those are the six tenses of English. However, the English verb also marks various other inflectional categories, as follows.

---

[1] I am grateful to an anonymous reader of the first draft for this example.

English has a CONTINUOUS (or PROGRESSIVE) aspect, which indicates that the action of the verb continues for some time. Continuous forms of the verb are constructed with the auxiliary verb 'be' followed by the PRESENT PARTICIPLE, which ends in *-ing*. There are continuous forms for all six tenses:

They are building the bridge.

They were building the bridge when the earthquake occurred.

A month from now that road will be closed because they will be building the bridge.

They have been building that bridge for a year and a half.

They had been building the bridge for only a couple of months when the workmen went on strike.

I guess by the time I die they will have been building that bridge for decades, and I bet they still won't have finished it.

The distinction between the English continuous present and simple present is complex and subtle. For the most part we use the continuous present to describe actions going on at the time of speaking, but the simple present to describe actions that happen repeatedly or are always true. So we say:

I go to the store every Wednesday.

Whenever I run out of something I just go to the store down the block.

But if someone runs into us on the street and asks us where we're going, we say

Right now I'm going to the store.

We don't say, and probably can't say

*Right now I go to the store.

That sounds like a sentence produced by a foreigner with an imperfect command of the language. However, there are a few verbs, including *see* and *know*, that we rarely use in the continuous present, even when talking about present time. We don't normally say

(*)I'm seeing the bridge.

If you say that, you imply that you're dating the bridge, or maybe that the bridge is your regular psychiatrist – two meanings of *see* which are quite different from the basic meaning. To use the present progressive of this verb in its basic meaning you need a very specific context, e.g.:

I can't figure out what I'm seeing here.

That works because you're implying that you keep seeing something and keep being unable to figure out what it is. This is a major hidden complexity of English grammar, one that is naturally difficult for a non-native speaker to learn. Comparison with Spanish, the other one of our languages that has a similar construction, shows that the list of verbs that do not usually appear in the continuous aspect is partly idiosyncratic. For instance, whereas

*I'm knowing / *estoy sabiendo

is equally weird in English and in Spanish, it is possible to say in Spanish (example from Butt and Benjamin 2011: 238):

Estoy viendo que vamos a acabar mal.

– literally, 'I'm seeing that we go to end badly', whereas in English we can only say 'I see that we're going to end badly.' (See further the following lesson.)

We now have no fewer than three auxiliary verbs in play, and we need to begin describing the English verb complex. The order of auxiliary verbs is fixed: it is always *will*, then *have*, then *be*. The future auxiliary *will* has only a single form (though see further below). Otherwise, whichever verb comes first is inflected for present or past tense. If there is no auxiliary, the main verb is present or past; if the aspect is continuous but there is no future or perfect auxiliary, *be* is present or past; if the verb is in a perfect tense, but not future perfect, *have* is present or past. Moreover, whatever immediately follows *have* must be a past participle, regardless of whether it is the main verb or the auxiliary *be*; and whatever follows *be* (which, so far, is always the main verb) must be a present participle. The whole system can be diagrammed as follows:

TENSE→ (will) (have + PASTPTC→) (be + PRESPTC→) MAINVERB

The parentheses mean that an item is optional – you always have a main verb, and the first item always carries a tense marker, but you don't always have an auxiliary. The arrows mean that a marker is applied to whatever item follows next: after *be* the next item is a present participle, after *have* it is a past participle, and the first item is always tensed – except that there is no past tense of *will*.

Or is there? A plausible past tense of *will* is *would*. Note the following pair of sentences:

> *If you climb up there you will see it.*
> *If you climbed up there you would see it.*

The first sentence has a subordinate clause in the present tense and a main clause in the future tense. The second sentence has a subordinate clause in the past tense and a main clause in what looks like the past of a future. In many languages such a form is called a CONDITIONAL TENSE, and we might as well use the term for English. Of course the past tense in the second sentence doesn't literally refer to the past; it's COUNTERFACTUAL. The clause means, in effect, 'If you were to climb up there (but you haven't), ...' Like some other languages, English regularly uses its past and pluperfect tenses as counterfactuals in clauses introduced by *if*, called CONDITIONAL CLAUSES.[2]

So the diagram above is completely accurate; there is even a past tense of *will*, although it doesn't usually mean 'was going to'. But there is one final piece of the picture. The auxiliary *be* is used not only to make progressive tenses, but also to construct passives (see Lesson 10). The verb phrase of a passive sentence is marked by the auxiliary *be* followed by a past participle. It turns out that if there is more than one auxiliary, the passive auxiliary is always last; so we can revise our diagram to read:

TENSE→ (will) (have + PASTPTC→) (be + PRESPTC→) (be + PASTPTC→) MAINVERB

All four auxiliaries can be present in a single clause, although it doesn't happen often. We can list all the possibilities with *see:*

---

[2] The use of the term "conditional" both for a specific verb form and for a type of clause is admittedly confusing; you should be careful to distinguish the two uses.

see	*will have seen*	*be being seen*
saw	*would have seen*	*was being seen*
will see	*will be seeing*	*will have been seeing*
would see	*would be seeing*	*would have been seeing*
have seen	*will be seen*	*will have been seen*
had seen	*would be seen*	*would have been seen*
be seeing	*have been seeing*	*will be being seen*
was seeing	*had been seeing*	*would be being seen*
be seen	*have been seen*	*have been being seen*
was seen	*had been seen*	*had been being seen*
		will have been being seen
		would have been being seen

– thirty-two phrases in all.[3] English verb inflection is simple, in the sense that each of the pieces doesn't have much inflection, but the auxiliary system makes large and complex verb phrases possible.

There are also several other items that occupy the same slot in the template as *will* and *would*, and most of them seem to be present-and-past-tense pairs: *shall* and *should*, *can* and *could*, *may* and *might*; only *must* isn't paired. These items (including *will* and *would*) are called MODAL VERBS. However, most modals don't express tense or aspect; they have meanings more like those of main verbs or phrases. (For instance, *can* means more or less the same thing as *be able to*.) In other words, English mixes up its tense-marking with other things, using the same machinery – modals – sometimes to express core categories of its verb inflection and sometimes to express more concrete meanings. That is unfortunately fairly typical of natural human languages. The meanings of the other modals are beyond the scope of this book.

Finally, we should say a little more about the forms of main verbs and auxiliaries. English verbs other than modals normally have up to five forms: a basic form which is identical with the root and which is used for most forms of the present tense; a 3sg. present form ending in *-(e)s* (see Lesson 5); a present

---

[3] In colloquial English, passive *be* – but not continuous *be* – can be replaced by *get*. However, that seldom occurs when the passive auxiliary is preceded by other auxiliaries. Someone should investigate that phenomenon.

participle ending in *-ing*, which is always completely regular; a past tense form, which for many common verbs is irregular; and a past participle, which is likewise often irregular. For regular verbs, the past and past participle are identical in shape, both ending in *-(e)d*, and even for many irregular verbs they are identical (*heard, kept, hit*), although for others they are not (*gave* vs. *given, sang* vs. *sung, saw* vs. *seen*, etc.). Only the verb 'be', both as main verb and as auxiliary, has a larger number of forms, which can be tabulated as follows:

root form: *be*

		present	past
sg.	1	*am*	*was*
	2	*are*	*were*
	3	*is*	*was*
pl.		*are*	*were*
participle		*being*	*been*

Like the 1st-person pronoun, this verb is suppletive. The only other suppletive verb in English is *go*; it has the usual number of forms, but its finite past *went* is completely unrelated in form to the others.

Further Reading

Gelderen 2002: 97–107 gives a brief description of the English verb system comparable to this one; Quirk et al. 1980: 61–122 treat the system in great detail. Comrie 1976 is the standard handbook on aspect and its relation to tense; it is highly relevant to this and the next five lessons.

15 | Tense, Aspect, and Mood: The Spanish Verb System

The Spanish verb system makes less use of auxiliaries than the English system does. Instead of only two simple tenses (present and past), there are five: present, IMPERFECT, PRETERITE, future, and conditional. Although the future and conditional are not constructed with auxiliaries, they translate the corresponding English tenses fairly straightforwardly:

> *Verá el puente unos momentos*   'You will see the bridge shortly before
>   *antes de llegar.*   arriving.'
> *Vería el puente si se metiera allí.*   'You would see the bridge if you
>   stood over there.'

The future is also virtually always used where English would use the continuous future:

> *La gente hablará de ello muchos*   'People will be talking about it for many
>   *años.*   years.'

The present likewise has a wider range of use than the English present; in parallel with the future, it is usually used when English would use the continuous present:

Ahora veo el puente.	'Now I see the bridge.'
Hablo por teléfono ahora.	'I'm talking on the phone now.'
Voy a la tienda.	'I'm going to the store.'
Construyen el puente.	'They are building the bridge.'

The two past tenses – the preterite and the imperfect – make an aspect distinction somewhat different from any that we make in English. The Spanish imperfect is a genuine IMPERFECTIVE aspect form: it indicates that the action had some structure which the speaker regards as important or relevant. Very often the action is continuous, so that the imperfect can often be translated by the English continuous past:

Hablaban de mí.   'They were talking about me.'

That's typically the case when an action was already in progress at the time something else happened:

Volvía a casa cuando encontré a Juan.	'I was returning home when I met John.'

Sometimes the action is one that was habitual in the past:

Decía que no había justicia en el mundo.	'He used to say that there was no justice in the world.'

However, states – being, having, staying, sleeping, and so on – that persisted over a period of time in the past are also expressed by the imperfect in Spanish, though we usually use the simple past for them in English:

Me quedaba tan solo en casa.	'I just stayed home.'
Tenía un coche rojo. Era muy divertido.	'I had a red car. It was lots of fun.'
Decía que no había justicia en el mundo.	'He used to say that there was no justice in the world.'

By contrast, the preterite simply indicates that something happened in the past:

Al doblar la esquina vi el puente.   'On turning the corner I saw the bridge.'

Not only is the speaker not interested in the internal structure of the action, (s)he implies that its internal structure (if any) is less important than the fact that the action occurred and was completed. In other words, the preterite is a past tense with PERFECTIVE aspect (as opposed both to the imperfect and to the English simple past – the latter leaves the aspect undetermined). Contrast the following two sentences:

Vivía allá mucho tiempo.	'He lived there for a long time.'	(imperfect)
Vivió setenta años.	'He lived for seventy years.'	(preterite: what's important to the speaker is the age that he attained)

As we will see in the next lesson, this distinction was inherited intact from Latin.

Like English, Spanish also has anterior tenses formed with the auxiliary verb *haber* (which is just an auxiliary, used for nothing else) and the past participle:

He visto la Alhambra.	'I have seen the Alhambra.'
Nunca había visto tal tontería.	'She had never seen such silliness.'
Lo habré acabado mañana.	'I will have finished it tomorrow.'

Although Spanish does have continuous tenses as well, formed with *estar* 'be' and the gerund (the form ending in *-ndo*) in much the same way as the English continuous tenses, they are used less often in Spanish. They emphasize that the action is ongoing at the relevant time – that is, they not only mark continuous aspect, they insist on it (as the English continuous tenses do not). So you can say

Está lloviendo.   'It's raining.'

if the rain has already started and is visible (see the discussion in Butt and Benjamin 2011: 233–35); but you would not use such a form in

Me dicen que llueve allí.	'They tell me that it's raining there.'
Parece que siempre llueve.	'It seems like it's always raining.'

Butt and Benjamin 2011: 233–40 explore the complexity of this construction in detail; note especially the restrictions spelled out on pp. 238–39.

Spanish expresses passives less uniformly than English does. You can make a passive with *ser* 'be' and the past participle, but in speech this construction tends to be avoided; an active sentence or a reflexive is usually used instead. See Lesson 10 for further discussion.

Spanish marks one grammatical category that has been lost in English, namely MOOD. Recall that in conditional sentences English uses the past and pluperfect tenses as counterfactuals in the *if*-clauses:

If you stood over there you would see it.
If you had stood over there you would have seen it.

Spanish has a special set of forms instead, part of the SUBJUNCTIVE mood:

Si se metiera allí, lo vería. ('if you were to place yourself there')
Si se hubiera metido allí, lo habría visto.

In some dialects of British and American English, at least, there is one subjunctive form still in productive use: many speakers still say *if I were* or *if (s)he were* as a counterfactual. Other dialects have abandoned even that relic, saying *if I was, if (s)he was* in the same circumstances.

The Spanish subjunctive has both present and past tenses, as well as anterior and (in principle) continuous tenses. They are used to express a wide variety of concepts, but never direct statements or questions; in general their use corresponds to the use of modals like *should, may*, and *might* in English.

With words meaning 'maybe, possibly' the subjunctive makes the statement weaker. In addition, the Spanish subjunctive is used in a wide range of subordinate clauses. Some uses are automatic, but sometimes there is a possible contrast between the indicative and subjunctive moods. When there is, the subjunctive usually indicates uncertainty or implies that the action indicated by the verb didn't or might not happen. For example:

Les pago cuando llegan.	'I (habitually) pay them when they arrive.'	(indicative)
Les pagaré cuando lleguen.	'I'll pay them whenever they arrive.'	(subjunctive)
Voy a comprar los zapatos que me gustan.	'I'm going to buy the shoes that I like.'	(indicative; implies that I've already identified them)

> *Voy a comprar los*   'I'm going to buy   (subjunctive)
> *zapatos que me*   whichever shoes
> *gusten.*   I like.'

Spanish also has an imperative mood for giving commands (something we do with the basic form in English). However, there are only 2nd-person familiar forms; if you want to be polite you have to use the present subjunctive instead. So you can tell a small child

> *Abre la ventana.*   'Open the window.'

but speaking to almost anyone else you would say

> *Abra (usted) la ventana (por favor).*   'Open the window (please).'

(The sentence is especially polite if you actually include the pronoun *usted*.) In addition, the subjunctive is used in negative commands, commands in the 3rd person, and 1st-person exhortations:

> *No abras la*   (familiar) / *No abra usted la*   (polite) 'Don't open the
> *ventana.*   *ventana.*   window.'
> *Si tiene hambre,* 'If (s)he's hungry, let him/her eat.'
> *coma.*
> *Comamos la*   'Let's eat dinner.'
> *cena.*

It is also used to express wishes, often preceded by a particle:

> *¡Ojalá no venga!*   'I hope (s)he doesn't come.'

Finally, note that every tense of the INDICATIVE (i.e. default) and subjunctive moods in Spanish has a full set of person-and-number forms for subject-verb agreement. Leaving aside the forms constructed with auxiliary verbs, the full paradigm of a regular Spanish verb looks like this. (Remember that the 2nd-person forms are familiar; the polite 2nd person agrees with a *3rd*-person verb.)

> infinitive   *comprar*   'to buy'   past participle   *comprado*   'bought'
> gerund   *comprando* 'buying'

		present indicative	present subjunctive	future
sg.	1	*compro*	*compre*	*compraré*
	2	*compras*	*compres*	*comprarás*
	3	*compra*	*compre*	*comprará*
pl.	1	*compramos*	*compremos*	*compraremos*
	2	*compráis*	*compréis*	*compraréis*
	3	*compran*	*compren*	*comprarán*

		imperfect	past subjunctive	conditional
sg.	1	*compraba*	*comprara*	*compraría*
	2	*comprabas*	*compraras*	*comprarías*
	3	*compraba*	*comprara*	*compraría*
pl.	1	*comprábamos*	*compráramos*	*compraríamos*
	2	*comprabais*	*comprarais*	*compraríais*
	3	*compraban*	*compraran*	*comprarían*

		preterite	imperative
sg.	1	*compré*	
	2	*compraste*	*compra*
	3	*compró*	
pl.	1	*compramos*	
	2	*comprasteis*	*comprad*
	3	*compraron*	

Although this paradigm is bound to seem large to a speaker of English, it is relatively transparent: it is easy to isolate the "pieces" that indicate particular grammatical categories. That is fairly typical of large paradigms, simply because it makes them easier to learn (although, unfortunately, such transparency is not universal).

Further Reading

Butt and Benjamin 2011: 166–327 (chapters 13 through 21) is a comprehensive and thorough description of the Spanish verb system and the uses of its grammatical categories, offering a wealth of further information on every point discussed here and on many more.

16 | The Latin Verb System

The Latin verb system resembles that of Spanish, its direct descendant. The most striking difference is that Latin makes very little use of auxiliaries: only *esse* 'to be', only to construct passive forms, and only in the perfect tenses – yet its system is actually larger than the Spanish system. Each verb therefore has a much larger number of actual forms.

To a surprising degree, the Latin system of tenses resembles that of English, but there is also some resemblance to the Spanish system. Latin appears to have six tenses, three simple and three anterior, just as in English; but one of the Latin tenses actually has two functions, which can be distinguished by its behavior in sentences. Corresponding to the English simple present, past, and future tenses are the Latin present, perfect, and future:

Pontem aedificant.	'They're building the bridge.' (present)
Pontem aedificāvērunt.	'They built the bridge.' (perfect)
Pontem aedificābunt.	'They will build the bridge.' (future)

Note that Latin has no continuous verb forms at all; an English or Spanish continuous form must be translated into Latin with the corresponding simple tense. However, like Spanish, Latin has a simple IMPERFECT tense, which is an IMPERFECTIVE past; like the Spanish imperfect, it indicates that the action had some structure that the speaker regards as important or relevant. The action might have been continuous:

Dē mē loquēbantur. 'They were talking about me.'

or it might have been going on when something else happened:

Domum <u>redībam</u> cum Mārcō obviam iī. '<u>I was returning</u> home when I met Marcus.'

or it might have been habitual:

<u>Dīcēbat</u> iūs in mundō exstāre nūllum. '<u>He used to say</u> that there was no justice in the world.'

As in Spanish, states that existed for some time in the past are expressed by the imperfect:

Domī modo <u>manēbam</u>. 'I just <u>stayed</u> home.'
Illīc diū <u>vīvēbat</u>. '<u>He lived</u> there for a long time.'

Also as in Spanish, the perfect (in its simple function, as exemplified above) is PERFECTIVE by contrast, emphasizing that an action occurred without calling attention to any internal structure that it might have had:

Septuāgintā annōs <u>vīxit</u>.   '<u>He lived</u> for seventy years.'

Like English, Latin also has anterior tenses, but they are single forms, not phrases. Nevertheless the Latin perfect, pluperfect, and future perfect correspond to the English present perfect, pluperfect, and future perfect fairly closely:

Parthenōnem Athēnīs <u>vīdī</u>.	'<u>I have seen</u> the Parthenon at Athens.'
Tantam stultitiam numquam <u>vīderat</u>.	'<u>She had</u> never <u>seen</u> such foolishness.'
Crās <u>cōnfēcerō</u>.	'<u>I will have finished</u> (it) tomorrow.'

Note that the perfect functions both as a simple (perfective) past and as an anterior tense corresponding to the English present perfect. You might suppose that its meaning is merely VAGUE – that is, it has a fairly broad range of meaning covering both concepts, like the English past tense in some dialects – and that only translation into another language forces us to specify one or the other. But it turns out that the meaning of the Latin perfect is AMBIGUOUS: it has two meanings which in some cases, at least, can actually be distinguished. Consider the following pair of sentences:

> *Lēgātōs ut cīvēs rem penitus intellegant mīsērunt.* 'They have sent envoys so that the citizens might understand the matter in detail.'
> *Lēgātōs ut cīvēs rem penitus intellegerent mīsērunt.* 'They sent envoys so that the citizens might understand the matter in detail.'

In the first sentence the main verb *mīsērunt* 'they (have) sent' selects a present subjunctive[1] *intellegant* in the subordinate clause; that forces an interpretation involving relevance to the present, so the correct English translation is present perfect 'they have sent'. In the second sentence it selects an imperfect subjunctive *intellegerent*, so the speaker is merely talking about something that happened in the past, and we should translate 'they sent'. It is remarkable that English marks the distinction in the main clause while Latin does so in the subordinate clause, but in either case the distinction is real; the Latin perfect really is ambiguous. That is unusual.

Like its descendant Spanish, Latin has three MOODS, called INDICATIVE (the default mood for statements and questions), SUBJUNCTIVE, and IMPERATIVE. The subjunctive has only four tenses – there are no future or future perfect subjunctives – and, as in Spanish, its functions are multiple and complex. The details are not always the same as in Spanish, but the system is roughly the same: the subjunctive usually expresses less certainty about an action than the indicative and can express that the action is merely hypothetical. It is used in counterfactual conditional sentences, e.g.:

> *Sī illīc cōnsisterēs, vidērēs.* 'If you were to stand there, you would see (it).'
> *Sī illīc cōnstitissēs, vīdissēs.* 'If you had stood there, you would have seen (it).'

Unlike Spanish, which has a separate conditional tense, Latin uses the same tense of the subjunctive in both clauses in sentences like these. In other uses the subjunctive often corresponds to phrases including modals like *should, may,* and

---

[1] See immediately below on the functions of the subjunctive.

might in English. With words meaning 'maybe, possibly' the subjunctive is usual. In addition, the Latin subjunctive is used in a wide range of subordinate clauses. Some uses are automatic, but sometimes there is a possible contrast between the indicative and subjunctive moods; when there is, the subjunctive usually indicates uncertainty or implies that the action indicated by the verb didn't or might not happen. For example:

> *Togam quae placet emam.* 'I'm going to buy the toga that (I) like.' (indicative; implies that I've already identified it)
> *Togam quae placeat emam.* 'I'm going to buy whichever toga (I) like.' (subjunctive)
> *Sīc facitō dum redībō.* 'Do so until I return.' (future indicative, because no waiting is involved)
> *Nihil facitō dum mē cōnsulās.* 'Do nothing until you consult me.' (subjunctive)

The Latin imperative is used for commands and requests much more than in Spanish because it is not considered impolite (although the subjunctive can also be used in polite requests).

A major difference between the Latin system and the Spanish and English systems is that Latin has single forms for the passive in the non-perfect tenses. For instance, here are the active and passive forms for the present indicative of 'see' (the passive means both 'be seen' and 'seem'):

		active		passive	
sg.	1	*videō*	'I see'	*videor*	'I am seen / seem'
	2	*vidēs*	'you (sg.) see'	*vidēris*	'you (sg.) are seen / seem'
	3	*videt*	'(s)he sees'	*vidētur*	'(s)he is seen / seems'
pl.	1	*vidēmus*	'we see'	*vidēmur*	'we are seen / seem'
	2	*vidētis*	'you (pl.) see'	*vidēminī*	'you (pl.) are seen / seem'
	3	*vident*	'they see'	*videntur*	'they are seen / seem'

The system is the same in the imperfect and the future. In all the perfect tenses, however, the passive forms are constructed with 'be' and the perfect participle, much as in Spanish or English. There is a difference, though: in the perfect passive, the tense of 'be' that is used is the *present* indicative, in the pluperfect passive the *imperfect* indicative, and so on. The Latin perfect participle really is perfect (i.e. anterior), not just passive, and it contributes its anterior meaning to the compound form. Here are the perfect active and passive of 'see':

		active		passive	
sg.	1	*vīdī*	'I saw'	*vīsus sum*	'I was seen / seemed'
	2	*vīdistī*	'you (sg.) saw'	*vīsus es*	'you (sg.) were seen / seemed'
	3	*vīdit*	'(s)he saw'	*vīsus/a est*[2]	'(s)he was seen / seemed'
pl.	1	*vīdimus*	'we saw'	*vīsī sumus*	'we were seen / seemed'
	2	*vīdistis*	'you (pl.) saw'	*vīsī estis*	'you (pl.) were seen / seemed'
	3	*vīdērunt*	'they saw'	*vīsī sunt*	'they were seen / seemed'

There is also a difference between the way a Latin verb paradigm is constructed and the way a Spanish verb paradigm is constructed. The forms of a Spanish regular verb are constructed from a single STEM, a kind of basic form found by subtracting the various endings; verbs for which you have to learn extra stems (for the preterite, for instance, or for the future and conditional) are by definition irregular, and there are only a couple dozen in common use (although there are some small groups of verbs that exhibit quirks, and some otherwise regular verbs have irregular past participles). In Latin the system as a whole is much less regular, and it makes sense to learn three stems for each verb: a present stem (from which the simple tenses, including those of the subjunctive and imperative, are formed); a perfect stem (from which the active anterior tenses of the indicative and subjunctive are formed); and a "third stem," usually exemplified by the perfect participle (if there is one) or the supine,[3] from which

---

[2] Since the perfect participle is an adjective in complement position, it must agree in gender with the subject; 'she was seen' is *vīsa est* (fem.), while 'he was seen' is *vīsus est* (masc.) and 'it was seen' is *vīsum est* (neut.). The same options exist for all the other forms; I omit them here for simplicity's sake.

[3] This is a kind of specialized infinitive; we do not need to describe its use here. The term "third stem" is adopted from Aronoff 1994.

a handful of nonfinite forms are constructed. Here are the three stems of a dozen and a half common Latin verbs:

	present stem	perfect stem	supine
'think'	*putā-*	*putāv-*	*putātum*
'forbid'	*vetā-*	*vetu-*	*vetitum*
'stand'	*stā-*	*stet-*	*statum*
'have'	*habē-*	*habu-*	*habitum*
'see'	*vidē-*	*vīd-*	*vīsum*
'persuade'	*suādē-*	*suās-*	*suāsum*
'hear'	*audī-*	*audīv-*	*audītum*
'come'	*venī-*	*vēn-*	*ventum*
'make, do'	*faci-*	*fēc-*	*factum*
'shake'	*quati-*	*quass-*	*quassum*
'pour'	*funde-*	*fūd-*	*fūsum*
'pound'	*tunde-*	*tutud-*	*tūsum*
'beget'	*gigne-*	*genu-*	*genitum*
'say'	*dīce-*	*dīx-* (i.e. *dīcs-*)	*dictum*
'give'	*da-*	*ded-*	*datum*
'go'	*ī- ~ e-*	*i-*	*itum*
'carry'	*fer(e)-*	*tul-*	*lātum*
'be'	*es- ~ er- ~ s-*	*fu-*	fut. ptc. *futūrus*

As you can see, a major source of irregularity is how the present and perfect stems are matched up with each other, and this list does not exemplify every matching by a long shot. On the other hand, not all patterns are equally common. About half the verbs in the language inflect like 'think', and a fair number like 'hear' (parallel to 'think', but with a different stem-final vowel); the pattern of 'have' is also common. Many other patterns are followed by only a few verbs each, and of the verbs in the above list, 'stand', 'give', and 'go' are unique, while 'carry' and 'be' are not only unique but suppletive. The existence of uniquely inflected or suppletive verbs is also characteristic of Spanish and English, although in the modern languages there are fewer uniquely inflected verbs. Irregularities of this kind are typical of European languages.

Further Reading

Gildersleeve and Lodge 1895 describes the verb system and the uses of its categories in great detail, with numerous examples. The forms are described in an earlier section of the book and their syntax in later sections, so that one often has to search for the answer to a specific question; but there is an extensive index of grammatical terms and Latin words that makes searching easier. Pinkster 2015, ch. 7 offers a thorough discussion of Latin tenses and moods from a modern perspective. The discussion of the Latin verb system in Aronoff 1994 is also illuminating.

17 | The Hebrew Verb System: Aspect and Derivation

Unlike European languages, Biblical Hebrew does not mark tense on the verb; it marks only aspect. The time to which the sentence refers is inferred from the context. The aspect system is simple: there is an IMPERFECT, marking IMPERFECTIVE aspect, which calls attention to the internal structure or continuation of the action, and a PERFECT, marking PERFECTIVE aspect, which states that an action occurred without reference to its internal structure. In addition there are imperative forms, active and passive participles (i.e. verbal adjectives; see Lesson 25), and an INFINITIVE and verbal noun (see Lesson 24). Thus the inflectional system of the verb is simple in principle, even taking into account the fact that the person, number, and gender of the subject are marked on all the FINITE VERB FORMS (i.e. everything except the participles, infinitive, and verbal noun), and the paradigm is correspondingly small.

However, examination of an actual paradigm shows complications of various kinds. Here is the paradigm of a perfectly regular verb, *šāmar-* 'keep':

	perfect		imperfect		imperative
1sg.	*šāmartī* 'I (have) kept'		*ʾešmōr* 'I (will) keep'		–
2sg. masc.	*šāmartā*	etc.	*tišmōr*	etc.	*šəmōr* 'keep!'

	perfect	imperfect	imperative
2sg. fem.	šāmart	tišmərī	šimərī
3sg. masc.	šāmar	yišmōr	—
3sg. fem.	šāmərā	tišmōr	—
1pl.	šāmarnū	nišmōr	—
2pl. masc.	šəmartem	tišmərū	šimərū
2pl. fem.	šəmarten	tišmōrnā	šəmōrnā
3pl. masc.	šāmərū	yišmərū	—
3pl. fem.	šāmərū	tišmōrnā	—
active participle	šōmēr 'keeping'		
passive participle	šāmūr 'kept'		
infinitive[1]	šəmōr 'to keep'	verbal noun	šāmōr 'keeping'

The perfect is inflected entirely by suffixes; the imperfect is inflected by a combination of prefixes and suffixes; the imperative is inflected only by suffixes, but they are the suffixes of the imperfect, not of the perfect. In addition, the vowels in the root of the verb (i.e. the part that indicates its lexical meaning, in this case 'keep') vary according to inflectional category. Only the perfect STEM (i.e. the basic form to which the endings are added) is šāmar-; the imperfect stem is -šmōr-; the imperative stem is šəmōr-; and each of the nonfinite forms has yet another set of vowels in the root. Thus a large part of the system involves ablaut, i.e. the systematic alternation of vowels in the root (see Lesson 10). Of course ablaut is also known from European languages: English verbs like sing (past sang, past participle sung) are obviously ablauting, and there are a handful of Latin and Spanish examples (e.g. Latin capere 'to take': cēpisse 'to have taken'). But in the European languages those are irregular verbs; in Hebrew all verbs are ablauting verbs. Moreover, although the pattern of vowels exemplified in the above paradigm is the default pattern, there are not a few verbs that exhibit other patterns. For all these reasons it is normal to cite Hebrew verbs only by giving their consonants; in a typical dictionary 'keep' will be listed as šmr.

---

[1] In traditional grammars this is called the "construct infinitive", while the verbal noun is called the "absolute infinitive"; the terms used here are more closely in accord with the grammatical terminology used for other languages.

In addition, the vowels of verb paradigms are often altered by PHONOLOGICAL RULES, which replace one sound by another not on the basis of the grammar, but simply on the basis of what other sounds they are adjacent to. In the paradigm above, some vowels are replaced by *ə* if they are followed by a sequence of consonant-plus-vowel and are in a maximally unstressed position (not marked in this quick survey); that is one of the simpler phonological rules of Hebrew. There are many others that affect the shapes of verb forms. For instance, to the perfect *nātan* 'he has given' corresponds imperfect *yittēn* 'he gives'; you might expect it to be **yintēn*, but in Hebrew an *n* ASSIMILATES to (i.e. becomes identical with) many following consonants. The consonants ', *h*, *ḥ*, ', *w*, and *y* also trigger or are affected by phonological rules that alter the shape of verb forms, sometimes drastically.

A further complication is caused by object pronouns. As we saw in Lesson 6, pronouns that indicate a direct object can be suffixed directly to the verb in Hebrew; as you might expect, they interact with the verb endings in complex ways, especially in the perfect.

Finally, Hebrew has an elaborate system for deriving verbs from other verbs. There are six regular derived patterns (plus some rare ones). Only one verb, *pqd* 'visit', makes all six; unfortunately, the meanings of its derived stems are idiosyncratic and opaque. The system can best be illustrated with two verbs, as follows.

	imperfect 3sg. masc.	perfect 3sg. masc.
šbr 'break':		
basic	*šābar* 'he broke'	*yišbōr* 'he breaks / will break'
passive	*nišbar* 'it was broken'	*yiššābēr* 'it is / will be broken'
intensive	*šibbēr* 'he smashed'	*yəšabbēr* 'he smashes / will smash'
intensive passive	*šubbar* 'it was smashed'	*yəšubbar* 'it is / will be smashed'
qdš 'be holy':		
basic	*qādaš* 'he is sacred'[2]	*yiqdōš* 'he will be sacred'
causative	*hiqdīš* 'he sanctified'	*yaqdīš* 'he will sanctify'

---

[2] Perfectives of stative verbs are often used for the present; see further below.

| causative passive | *huqdaš* 'he was sanctified' | *yuqdaš* 'he will be sanctified' |
| reflexive | *hiṯqaddēš* 'he sanctified himself' | *yiṯqaddēš* 'he will sanctify himself' |

Each derived verb type has a full paradigm of its own, sometimes with affixes somewhat different from those of basic verbs.

The "intensive" stems actually have a variety of meanings, depending on the identity of the basic verb; they can indicate plural action, or be causative, for example.[3] That is one of the indications that this system is not simply part of the inflection of a single verb: words derived from other words acquire a life of their own, so to speak, and their meanings can develop independently, whereas members of a single paradigm usually retain a single meaning, or the same set of meanings. The other indication that this is a derivational system is that it has numerous gaps: many basic verbs have several derivatives, but only *pqd* 'visit' has all seven. A considerable number of verbs occur only in one or more of the derived paradigms, having no attested basic form. By contrast, although gaps in inflectional paradigms do occasionally occur, they are quite rare.

The Hebrew verb system will be unfamiliar enough to most readers that it is likely to raise several questions, at least a couple of which should be answered here. As I noted above, the system is UNDERLYINGLY simple – that is, it expresses only a few basic grammatical notions – but is greatly complicated by phonological rules and by many irregularities in detail. How typical of human languages is that? In fact, it's typical enough that this is not the only example known to me. Both Old English (the stage of English before the Norman Conquest, sometimes called Anglo-Saxon) and Old Norse (the language in which the Icelandic sagas are written) also have under-lyingly simple grammars – especially verb systems – that are made much harder to learn by pervasive phonological rules and a welter of irregularities. Moreover, it is also possible for a language to have an underlyingly complex grammar – again, especially a complex verb system – that is made even more complex by irregular-ities and phonological rules. As you can see from the next lesson, Navajo is such a language; Old Irish (i.e. early mediaeval Irish Gaelic) is another.

Perhaps more importantly, how does a language that does not mark tense on its verbs avoid making statements that are ambiguous with respect to the time at

---

[3] I am grateful to Aaron Rubin for helpful discussion of this point.

which they occur? Somewhat surprisingly, there is hardly ever any ambiguity in practice, because the context in which an aspect-marking verb form occurs usually makes it clear what time the speaker is talking about. To begin with, perfective verb forms cannot be used to talk about the present unless they are statives (like 'be holy' above, or 'know' in the example below), because if something is going on *while* the speaker is talking, it necessarily has an internal structure that can't be ignored (see the discussion in Lesson 14). Thus most perfectives can be used only to talk about the past or the future. In practice most perfectives refer to the past, and that is why I have translated Hebrew perfects by English present perfects and pasts in this lesson. But stative perfects can refer to the present, e.g. in *Genesis* 4.9:

> *Wayyōmer YHWH* [4] *'el-Qayin, 'Ē Heḇel 'āḥīḵā? Wayyōmer, Lō yāḏa'tī.*
> 'And the Lord said to Cain, where (is) Abel your brother? And he said, <u>I do not know.</u>'

To express continuous action in the past, when it is not clear from the context, Hebrew resorts to another device: it uses the active participle, with the verb 'be' understood. We have already seen an example toward the end of Lesson 8:

> *... wərūᵃḥ ᵉlōhīm ___ məraḥep̄eṭ 'al-pənē hammāyim.*
> '... and the breath of God (<u>was</u>) wafting over the waters.'

(The participle *məraḥep̄eṭ* is feminine, agreeing in gender with the subject *rūᵃḥ*.) The same construction can be used to refer to continuous action at the time of speaking, and over the centuries the active participle gradually came to be the usual way of expressing present time with a verb in Hebrew.

Further Reading

A concise but comprehensive description of the Biblical Hebrew verb is Gesenius and Kautzsch 1910: 114–220 (the forms), 309–89 (the syntax). The discussion of the aspects on pp. 309–19 is a good orientation to the verb systems of Semitic languages in general.

---

[4] This is the given name of God in the Hebrew Bible; it is never pronounced, always being replaced by 'my Lord' in reading or quoting. Because pronouncing the name was tabu, the original pronunciation has been lost.

18 | The Navajo Verb System: Aspect, Tense, Mood, and Derivation

The inflection of the Navajo verb system, like that of Hebrew, is based primarily on aspect distinctions; but the system is much more complex, and future tense and OPTATIVE mood (used to express wishes) are also expressed by the aspect system. The inflectional categories along that parameter are:

IMPERFECTIVE, which calls attention to the internal structure of an action
PERFECTIVE, which simply mentions an action or state
USITATIVE, expressing habitual actions or actions customarily done
ITERATIVE, expressing actions repeated on separate occasions
PROGRESSIVE, expressing actions performed while moving along
FUTURE TENSE
OPTATIVE MOOD

"Active" verbs are inflected for all these categories. "Neuter" verbs are inflected only in the imperfective or only in the perfective; imperfective neuters are stative verbs indicating qualities (usually expressed by adjectives in English; see further Lesson 22), while perfective neuters are stative verbs indicating position (see the end of this lesson).

Here are the seven aspect forms of 'carry a living being' (a classificatory verb, see Lesson 12) with no derivational prefix, meaning specifically 'bring a living being', and 3rd-person subject and 3rd-person object:

ipf.	*yiłteeh*	'(s)he is/was bringing him/her'
pf.	*yiniłtį́*	'(s)he brought him/her'
us.	*yiłtééh*	'(s)he customarily brings / used to bring him/her'
it.	*néíłtééh*	'(s)he brings / brought him/her again and again'
prog.	*yoołtééł*	'(s)he is/was bringing him/her along'
fut.	*yidoołtééł*	'(s)he will bring him/her'
opt.	*yółtééł*	'let him/her bring him/her'

You can see that the prefixes are different for each of the categories; but the lexical part of the verb, which is the last syllable, also varies between *-teeh*, *-tééh*, *-tééł*, and *-tį́*. That is typical. In principle, each active verb has five stems: one each for the imperfective, perfective, and optative, a fourth stem for the usitative and iterative, and a fifth for the progressive and future. However, in many verbs two or more of those stems are identical in shape (in this case the optative stem and progressive stem are identical). Those variations are idiosyncratic and have to be learned for each verb. The prefixes are not idiosyncratic – they can usually be predicted from the meaning of the verb – but the number of distinct sets is very large.

As we saw in Lessons 5 and 6, Navajo has subject-verb agreement (although the agreement marker for 3rd-person subjects is zero) and also marks the direct object on the verb (although 3rd-person objects are marked only if the subject is also 3rd-person, and number is not marked for 3rd-person objects). Thus each of the aspect categories has a range of forms for different subjects and objects. The forms for the imperfective of this verb are, in part:

nishteeh 'I'm bringing him/her/them'
niłteeh 'you (sg.) are bringing him/her/them'
niilteeh 'we're bringing him/her/them'
nołteeh 'you (pl.) are bringing him/her/them'
shiłteeh '(s)he/they is/are bringing me'
niłteeh '(s)he/they is/are bringing you (sg.)'
nihiłteeh '(s)he/they is/are bringing us/you (pl.)'

The forms are less opaque than they seem. The verb stem is *-teeh*; it is preceded by a conjugation prefix *-ł-* (called the "classifier" in Athabaskan grammar) which marks many, though not all, transitive verbs. There is a prefix *ni-* that marks the imperfective in this and many other verbs (although there are also other imperfective prefixes). In the first four forms the subject pronouns are *-sh-* 'I', *-ni-* 'you (sg.)', *-iid-* 'we', and *-oh-* 'you (pl.)', following the imperfective prefix but preceding the classifier. The classifier *-ł-* is deleted after *-sh-*, but the *-h-* of *-oh-* is deleted before the classifier; the *-d-* of *-iid-* and the classifier *-ł-* merge into *-l-*. Finally, any syllable *-ni-* is replaced by high tone if it is preceded by a vowel and followed immediately by the classifier or stem; thus expected *ni-ni-ł-teeh 'you (sg.) are bringing him/her/them' surfaces as *níłteeh*. However, the object pronouns *precede* the imperfective prefix *ni-*, so they in turn cause it to become high tone: *shi-ni-ł-teeh surfaces and *shíłteeh*, and so on. Both the complexity of the system and the large number of phonological rules that affect prefixes make Navajo verb inflection formidably difficult to learn, even if we disregard the irregular formation of verb stems.

However, that is still not the whole story. Like Hebrew, Navajo has a system for deriving sets of related verbs; but whereas the Hebrew system is very modest in size, the Navajo system is vast. There are dozens of derivational prefixes that can appear first in the verb form; in addition, there are at least sixteen that appear *between* the direct object prefixes and the aspect prefixes, where they are affected by a range of phonological rules that can make them difficult to recognize and learn. Moreover, among the inflectional prefixes there are several that mark imperfective aspect and several that mark perfective aspect – and derivational prefixes typically each require one particular imperfective prefix and one particular perfective prefix. The result is a very large number of possible prefix complexes that must be learned.

Derivational prefixes mean a wide range of things, but many of them have meanings that can also be described as aspectual (see Young and Morgan 1980, grammar pp. 105–6 for a list and 326–45 for extended discussion). For instance, the paradigm of 'bring a living being' of which parts were given above is a MOMENTANEOUS paradigm, indicating that a living being is brought to a fixed point at a given time. There is also a CONTINUATIVE paradigm that occurs with the prefix *na-* 'around; to a destination and back', e.g.:

ipf.	*neiłté*	'(s)he is/was carrying him/her around'
pf.	*nasíłtį́*	'(s)he carried him/her (to a destination and back)'
us.	*neiłteeh*	'(s)he customarily carries / used to carry him/her (to a destination and back)'

it.	*nanéíłtééh*	'(s)he repeatedly carries / carried him/her (to a destination and back)'
fut.	*neidoołteeł*	'(s)he will bring him/her (to a destination and back)'
opt.	*naołtééł*	'let him/her carry him/her (to a destination and back)'

There are other derived aspect paradigms for this verb root.

Finally, there are unforeseen complications with individual sets of verbs. For instance, most neuter verbs inflected with the perfective prefix *si-* are classificatory verbs that indicate the shape of an object motionless in a position, e.g.:[1]

Naaltsoos   bikáá'adání   bikáa'gi   dah si'ą́.
(book/paper table   above-on up compact-object-lies-PERF)
'The book is lying on the table.'

Naaltsoos   bikáá'adání   bikáa'gi   dah siłtsooz.
(book/paper table   above-on up flat-flexible-object-lies-PERF)
'The sheet of paper is lying on the table.'

However, for animate objects a distinction is made between sitting, standing, and lying down (as in most languages) – and, exceptionally, the verb stems meaning 'sit' and 'lie' also indicate whether the subject is singular, dual, or plural. For instance:

sédá	'I'm sitting'
sínídá	'you (sg.) are sitting'
sidá	'(s)he is sitting'
siiké	'the two of us are sitting'
sooké	'the two of you are sitting'
siké	'the two of them are sitting'
nahísíitą́	'we (more than two) are sitting'
nahísóotą́	'you (more than two) are sitting'
naháaztą́	'they (more than two) are sitting'

A handful of other verbs relating to humans makes the same distinction; for instance, there are verbs meaning 'one person goes', 'two people go', 'many people go'.

If you are not trying to learn Navajo, the most important things to be learned from this very sketchy and superficial discussion of the Navajo verb system are

---

[1] These examples are from Young and Morgan 1980, grammar p. 300.

that verb inflection can be more complex and more irregular than you can (probably) imagine, and that it can express grammatical categories that you would (probably) not have thought of. Other systems of verb inflection that are notably large and/or irregular can be found in Bantu, Eskimo-Aleut, Algonkian, and Iroquoian languages, and in Georgian.

Further Reading

The standard reference for Navajo is Young and Morgan 1980, which contains both a
dictionary and a grammar. The verb system is described in grammar pp. 99–393
(with appendices pp. 394–471, describing the system of classificatory verbs and
listing verb stems and prefix complexes) and is also the subject of Young 2000. It is
vast, bewilderingly complex, and typical of the verb systems of Athabaskan
languages, although those spoken in Alaska have more transparent phonology.
A user-friendly introduction to the Navajo verb is Faltz 1998. On Navajo verb prefix
phonology, see also Kari 1976.

19 | The Mandarin Verb System: Aspect and Serial Verbs

The Mandarin verb system differs from all the systems sketched above in having no inflection: it uses particles of various kinds to express the same sorts of things expressed by inflectional markers, and their use is tightly rule-governed, as one would expect.

Like Hebrew and Navajo, Mandarin does not mark tense on the verb. As usual, that causes little ambiguity, both because the time of an action can very often be inferred from the context and because it is always possible to specify the time by an adverb such as *xiànzài* 现在 'now' or *zuótiān* 昨天 'yesterday'. Mandarin does mark aspect on the verb, although verbs are very often used with no aspect marker.

The most important aspect marker is COMPLETIVE *le* 了, which indicates that an action has been or will be completed. (It is sometimes loosely called "perfective," but I am using that term in a more comprehensive way – see the preceding lessons.) Very often a verb with *le* can be translated with an English past:

> *Wǒ chī le zǎofàn.* 我吃了早饭. 'I have eaten breakfast.' / 'I ate breakfast.'
> *Tā mǎi le liǎng zhāng piào.* 他买了兩张票. 'He/she bought two tickets.'

But a completed event in the future is also indicated by *le*:

Wǒ míngtiān xià le kè, yǐhòu kàn shū. 我明天下了课, 以後看书.
(I tomorrow   end COMP class, afterwards look-at book(s).)
'After I'm done with class tomorrow I'll read.'

And past events are not always marked by *le*:

Wǒ zuótiān kàn shū, jīntiān xiě xìn. 我昨天看书, 今天写信.
'Yesterday I read; today I'm writing letters.'

There is a special marker *guo* 过 to indicate past experience:

Nǐ chī guo Běijīng kǎoyā ma? 你吃过北京烤鸭吗?
'Have you (ever) eaten Peking duck?'
(Contrast: *Wǒ zuótiān chī le Běijīng kǎoyā.* 我昨天吃了北京烤鸭.
'Yesterday I ate Peking duck.')

The marker *zhe* 着 indicates that the action of the verb is subsidiary to another action (examples from Yip and Rimmington 1997: 45):

Lǎoshī   xiào   zhe shuō   "Xièxie."   老帅笑着说谢谢.
(teacher   smile   zhe say   "thanks")
'Smiling, the teacher said "Thank you."'

But the same marker is also used to indicate states resulting from an action:

"Kāi chuāng ba." – "Chuāng kāi zhe." 开窗吧. – 窗开着.
'"How about opening the window?" – "The window is open."'

There is also a marker *zài* 在, placed before the main verb, that indicates action in progress, much like the English continuous tenses. But whereas the other markers are particles, which cannot be used separately from a verb, *zài* is actually a verb in its own right, meaning 'be (in a place)'. Thus progressive phrases with *zài* are really examples of the Mandarin SERIAL VERB construction, in which two or more verbs are used together to express a single complex idea. Examples:

Wǒ zài dǎ diànhuà. 我在打电话. 'I am making a phone call.'
Háizi zài shuìjiào. 孩子在睡觉. 'The children are sleeping.'
Tā qùnián zài niàn dàxué. 他去年在念大学.
'Last year he was studying at the university.'

Other examples of the serial verb construction must be translated in very diverse ways, depending on the identities of the verbs used together, e.g.:

Nǐ   yào   xué   kāi   chē   ma?   你要学开车吗?
(you want learn operate vehicle ?)
'Do you want to learn how to drive a car?'

Wǒ   bú   huì   shuō   Pǔtōnghuà.   我不会说普通话.
(I   not   be-able speak Common-language.)
'I can't speak (standard) Mandarin.'

Some patterns of serial verbs must be in a fixed order which is not obvious from general considerations. The verbs *qù* 去 'go' and *lái* 来 'come' are used to indicate direction away from or toward the speaker and typically follow other verbs in the clause (Yip and Rimmington 1997: 48–52). For instance, a (very funny) popular song begins:

Duìmiàn   de nǚhái,   kàn guò lái!   对面的女孩, 看过来.
(opposite-side -'s girl(s), look cross come)
'Girls on the far side, look over here!'

If a verb of motion that takes an object precedes the directional verb, the latter must follow the object, e.g.:

Dàjiā   xià   lóu   lái.   大家下楼来.
(everyone   descend stairs come.)
'Everybody come downstairs!'

If they are combined with other verbs, *qù* and *lái* can have idiomatic meanings, e.g.:[1]

Tā   chàng qǐ   gē   lái. 她唱起歌来.   'She began to sing.'
(she   sing   rise song come.)

Qìchē tíng xiàlái   le.   汽车停下来了. 'The car gradually came to a
                                                stop.'

(car stop descend-come COMP.)

---

[1] These examples are from Yip and Rimmington 1997: 51–52.

Qǐng shuō xiàqù.   请说下去.   'Please continue (speaking).'
(please speak descend-go.)

As you can see, some of the verbs used in serial constructions resemble English modals in meaning. However, all are part of the same complexly structured system; there are constraints on what order the elements appear in, but there is no special class of verbs like the English modals.

Further Reading

A concise and convenient introduction to the Mandarin verb system is Yip and Rimmington 1997: 29–92, with a discussion of serial verb constructions pp. 125–31.

20 | Negation

In principle negation is a simple matter: you simply need a word or affix meaning 'not' and a rule for where to put it. In practice, languages usually do things more complexly, although there is a strong tendency to place the item meaning 'not' immediately before the item that it negates.

As usual, Mandarin has a simple and transparent system, but even Mandarin introduces a couple of simple quirks. The usual word for 'not' is *bù* 不, and it is usually placed immediately before whatever it negates:

> *Bù zhīdào.* 不知道. '(I) don't know.'
> *bù shǎo shū* 不少书 'not a few books', i.e. 'a fairly large number of books'
> *Tā chī bù bǎo.* 他吃不饱. 'He couldn't eat his fill.'
> (he eat not sated)
>
> (Yip and Rimmington 1997: 71.)

The position of the negative matters (Yip and Rimmington 1997: 85):

> *Wǒ jīntiān bù néng lái.* 我今天不能来. 'I can't come today.' (*néng* 'be able to')
> *Wǒ jīntiān néng bù lái ma?* 我今天能不来吗. 'Can I not come today?'
> —i.e. 'Do I have to come today?'

Multiple negatives are interpreted independently (Yip and Rimmington 1997: 85):

Nǐ bù néng bù lái. 你不能不来. 'You're not capable of not coming.'

However, the verb *yǒu* 'have' is negated by *méi:*

Wǒ méi yǒu qìchē. 我没有汽车. 'I don't have a car.'

Because *méi* has no other use, it can be used by itself colloquially to mean 'don't have' – the speaker can supply *yǒu* because that's the only thing that could follow it! Negative commands are introduced by *bú yào*,[1] literally 'don't want (to)':

Bú yào dòng! 不要动! 'Don't move!'

The phrase can be contracted to *bié:*

Bié dòng! 别动! 'Don't move!'

In spite of these quirks, the system is so straightforward that Yip and Rimmington 1997 don't even have a section on negation.

Navajo negation is also simple, dealt with on one page (grammar p. 352) in Young and Morgan 1980. The usual negative is *doo . . . da*; it is unusual in that it brackets the phrase that is negated, e.g.:

Doo łá 'ájíníi da. 'Don't joke around.'

The example shows that it can be used in commands, in keeping with the principle that there is nothing grammatically special about commands in Navajo.

Spanish negation is only a little more complex. The word for 'not' is *no*, and it is placed immediately before what it negates, except that it cannot separate an unstressed object pronoun from the verb that governs it. The following examples[2] are typical:

No intento perder tiempo. 'I'm not trying to waste time.'
Intento no perder tiempo. 'I'm trying not to waste time.'
No todos son capaces de hacerlo. 'Not everyone is able to do it.'
No lo he visto. 'I haven't seen him.' (*lo* 'him', unstressed)

---

[1] Before a word with the 4th (falling) tone, the 4th tone of *bù* is shifted to 2nd (rising). That is a purely phonological rule, i.e. a rule of pronunciation: it has nothing to do with the meaning of either word.

[2] These are adapted from Butt and Benjamin 2011: 336–37.

The main complication is that Spanish has a rule of NEGATIVE CONCORD. The main negative of the clause is copied rightward onto words that translate English *any* and its compounds. Note the following sentences:

Nadie vino. 'No one came.'
No   vino   nadie. 'No one came.'
(not came no-one)
No   veo   nadie. 'I don't see anyone.'
(not I-see no-one)
No   dijo   nada. 'He didn't say anything.'
(not he-said nothing)
Nadie   dijo nada. 'No one said anything.'
(no-one said nothing)

Usually the negative that gets copied is the sentential negative *no*, but other negatives can also be copied rightward (as the last example shows). However, if *no* is present, it can only be copied rightward, not leftward:

No vino nadie.

is normal, but one does not say

*Nadie no vino.

even though *nadie* is the subject; one says *Nadie vino*, which means the same thing. This is *exactly* like the negative copying rule of Ancient Greek, standard Italian, and nonstandard English dialects (on which see below). It is important to realize that the negatives are not independent and cannot be interpreted independently; the ones to the right are just meaningless copies of the leftmost negative. Most of the negative words begin with *n-* and were originally compounds of 'not' and something else; other examples are *nunca* 'never' and *ni . . . ni* 'neither . . . nor'.

A further peculiarity of Spanish is that one cannot use *no* with imperatives. Of course, the imperative has only 2nd-person familiar forms, but even to a small child you cannot say

*¡No lo haz!

– it's just ungrammatical. You have to use the subjunctive and say

¡No lo hagas! 'Don't do it.'

(The polite form would be: *¡No lo haga usted!*)

Latin, the direct ancestor of Spanish, has a more complex system of negatives. The default negative is *nōn*, and (as expected) it usually precedes what it negates. However, there is also a negative *nē* which is used in wishes, polite commands in the subjunctive (cf. Spanish above), and some types of subordinate clauses:

Nōn est vīvere, sed valēre, vīta. 'Not living, but being well, is life.'
> (Martial VI.70.15, cited by Gildersleeve and Lodge 1895: 287)

Nē vīvam sī sciō. 'May I not live if I know.'
> (Cicero, *Letters to Atticus* IV.16.8, cited ibid. p. 288)

In subordinate clauses *nē* can function both as a negative and as the CONJUNCTION that introduces the clause, e.g.:

Cūrā nē cadās. 'Take care <u>that</u> you <u>don't</u> fall.'

Latin has a good many conjunction-plus-negative combinations, including *neque ~ nec* 'and not, nor', which follows *nōn*; *nēve ~ neu* 'and not, nor', which follows *nē*; *nisi ~ nī* 'unless', i.e. 'if not':

Nōn sciō, nec scīre studeō. 'I don't know, <u>and</u> I'm <u>not</u> eager to know.'
Nē illam vēndās neu mē perdās hominem amantem. 'Please don't sell her <u>and</u> (<u>don't</u>) destroy me, a guy in love.'
> (Plautus, *Pseudolus* 322, cited ibid. p. 288)

There are also negative compounds like those of Spanish, e.g. *nēmō* 'no one', *nihil* 'nothing', *numquam* 'never'; Latin has many more.

What Latin does not have is negative concord of any kind; in that respect it is like German or the standard dialects of English. "Two negatives in the same sentence destroy one another, and make an affirmative" (Gildersleeve and Lodge 1895: 289):

Quī mortem in malīs pōnit nōn potest eam nōn timēre. 'He who puts death among the evils is <u>not</u> able <u>not</u> to fear it.'

Latin does have NEGATIVE POLARITY ITEMS, which are used mainly in negative clauses and questions, and in comparative constructions. A typical example is *ūllus* 'any':

Hoc facere nōn audeō, nec <u>ūllō</u> modō possim. 'I don't dare do that, <u>and</u>
I <u>couldn't</u> by <u>any</u> means.'

Potestne <u>ūllō</u> modō fierī? 'Can it be done by <u>any</u> means?'

<u>ūllā</u> nive candidior 'whiter than <u>any</u> snow'

There are typically negative compounds of such items, in this case *nūllus* 'no,
none':

Nūllō modō fierī potest. 'By no means can it be done.' = 'It can't be done by
any means.'

All these details are mirrored in the standard dialects of English (see
further below).

Like Spanish, Latin does not usually use negatives with imperatives (although it
can be done in poetry). The usual alternative is to use the imperative of *nōlle* 'to
not want, to be unwilling', a negative compound of *velle* 'to want, to be willing':

Nōlī hoc facere! 'Don't do this!' ('Be unwilling to do this!')

That construction is more or less identical with Mandarin *bú yào*, although there
is no historical connection between them. It is also possible to use *nē* with the
perfect subjunctive. A typical example is

Nē crēdiderīs! 'Don't believe it!'

As in Spanish, the present subjunctive can be used for more polite commands
(cf. the quotation from Plautus above), and in that case *nē* is used (*nē hoc faciās*;
nē crēdās).

Biblical Hebrew has a simple negative system: *lō'* 'not' precedes what it
negates, much as in Mandarin. However, like Spanish and Latin, Hebrew does
not use the negative with imperatives; a negative command must be in the
imperfect. Moreover, there is a special negative particle *'al* used in commands:

<u>Šəmōr</u> 'et-dəbāray. '<u>Keep</u> my words.' (imperative)

'Al <u>tišmōr</u> 'et-dibrēhem. 'Do not <u>keep</u> their words.' (imperfect)

In addition, there is a special negative existential *'ēn* 'there is not' corresponding
to *yēš* 'there is'.

English has the most complex negative system of all. Whether there is
negative concord depends on the dialect. Many nonstandard dialects have

left-to-right negative concord. For instance, in the Appalachian vernacular one can say either

Nobody came.

or

Didn't nobody come.

(but not **Nobody didn't come.*), and it's normal to say

Cain't nobody do nothin' about it. 'No one can do anything about it.'

In this detail the nonstandard dialects are actually more conservative than the standard ones. If you learn to read the works of Chaucer (who died in 1400) in the original, you will find that he too has negative concord, although for him the sentential negative *ne* can be anywhere in the clause, e.g.:

He never yet no vileinye ne sayde	'He never yet said anything base
in al his lyf, unto no maner wight.	in all his life, to any sort of creature.'

(Canterbury Tales, Prologue 70–71)

In the centuries since then standard English has changed completely in this regard; the nonstandard dialects have changed much less. In the standard dialect, and in other dialects that do not have negative concord, there are negative polarity items, typically *any* and its compounds; the translations above illustrate how the system works. As in Latin, two negatives cancel each other out in those dialects because neither can be a copy; the translation *is not able not to fear it* (see above) is typical. You can see from this discussion that the schoolroom stigmatization of double negatives as "bad grammar" is very wide of the mark. (On the concept of "bad grammar," see the Epilogue.)

But there are three other peculiarities that make English negation even more complex than that of Latin. The first involves the position of the negative. For the most part the English negative *not* precedes what it negates, just like Mandarin *bù*, Spanish *no*, and Latin *nōn*. We can say

He changed his mind not many days later. (i.e. a few days later)

and, as in the translation above,

. . . not to fear it. (or, in colloquial American English, *to not fear it.*)

But look again at the sentence

He is not able not to fear it.

The first *not* doesn't precede the verb *is*: it follows it. That is a systematic exception to the general rule that negatives precede: *not* cannot precede the tensed verb in English (see Lesson 14); it must follow it. Compare the following sentences in Latin, Mandarin, Spanish, Hebrew, and English, which translate one another:

Nōn vīdī.
Wǒ bú kànjiàn guo.
No lo he visto.
Lō rəʾīṯīhū.
I have not seen it.

In all the other languages the negative (*nōn / bú / no / lō*) precedes the tensed verb (*vīdī / kànjiàn / he / rāʾīṯī*), but in English it follows, appearing between the tensed auxiliary and the participle *seen*.

That is fairly straightforward, but the second complication is much worse. The English negative *not* regularly appears after the first auxiliary in the verb complex, e.g.:

His house [will not have been being built] for very long when he runs out of money.

However, it cannot appear after a main verb; **he knows not* is completely ungrammatical in modern English. That was not the case five centuries ago. It's alleged that in the 1530s Catherine Howard, a future wife of King Henry VIII, had an affair with Francis Dereham (a secretary in the aristocratic household where she was being brought up) at the age of 13 or so and addressed him as "husband"; another well-born girl who slept in the same dormitory was shocked and said that Catherine

knew not what matrimony was.

(Weir 1991: 446)

In Modern English we would have to say

she didn't know what matrimony was.

The rule is simply stated: if there is no auxiliary verb, insert an auxiliary *do* and follow the usual rules (tense marked on the auxiliary, *not* immediately following). But so far as I can discover, no other language does that – and that makes English much harder to learn as a second language.

The "*do*-insertion" rule was optional for generations, and there is still an exception or two. Shakespeare, in the decades around 1600, can still write

> *Alas, I <u>blame you not</u>,*[3] *for you are mortal,*
>
> > (*Richard III* 1.2)

but in the same scene he can also write

> *I <u>did not kill</u> your husband.*

In Modern English *not* still follows the verb 'be', even when it is not an auxiliary. We say

> *They <u>are not</u> able to do it.*

In fact we can't say

> **They don't be able to do it.*

– there is no optionality; *be* is just an exception. In conservative dialects of British English *have* behaves the same way, even when it is not an auxiliary. One says

> *We haven't any reason to do that.*

whereas Americans, and some Britons, would say

> *We don't have any reason to do that.*

Of course these exceptions complicate the situation further.

English *not* can (and in speech usually does) contract with most preceding auxiliaries (and with *be*, whether or not it is an auxiliary), and some of the contractions are very irregular. *Shouldn't* is straightforwardly derivable from *should not*, but *won't* for *will not* is simply a form that has to be memorized, and even *don't*, although it is spelled normally, has a vowel different from *do* in all standard dialects of English.

---

[3] Note that in Shakespeare's English, as in Spanish, the unstressed object pronoun cannot be separated from its verb, so that the negative has to be placed "outside" that phrase; only the word order is different.

Finally, negative SCOPE in English is not as straightforward as in our other languages. In Navajo a negative negates only what it brackets, and in Mandarin, Latin, Spanish, and Hebrew it negates only what follows it, but for some speakers of English a negative can negate something that precedes it. Consider the following set of sentences. All speakers of English would probably agree that

Not all the arrows hit the target.

implies that some did and some didn't (otherwise why not say *No arrows . . . ?*), because *not* takes scope over *all* and negates it. For some speakers of English

All the arrows didn't hit the target.

implies that none did, because *all* takes scope over *not*. It means the same thing as

All the arrows failed to hit the target.

But for other speakers of English, the sentence

All the arrows didn't hit the target.

is ambiguous: it might mean that none of them did, but it might also mean that not all of them did – just like the first sentence. For those speakers, *not* can take scope over *all*, even though *all* is at the beginning of the sentence. That's probably not unique to English, but it is definitely unusual.

Exercise

Here are some Old English sentences (from about the year 1000, before the Norman Conquest). What can you infer about negation in English at that date?

Ne   cann iċ nāht   singan.
(not   know I   nothing sing-INF)
'I don't know how to sing anything.'
. . . for þon iċ nāht   singan   ne   cūþe.
   (because I   nothing sing-INF not know-PAST)
'. . . because I didn't know how to sing anything.'

Heora *nān* *nyste*   *hwæt ōþer cwæþ.*
(they-GEN none not-know-PAST what other say-PAST)
'None of them knew what another was saying.'
Nis *þē*   *nān þing earfoþe.*
(not-is you-DAT no thing difficulty-DAT)
'Nothing is hard for you.'

To Be Remembered from Lesson 20

1 Whether or not a language has negative concord has to be learned separately
for each language (or, in some cases, each dialect of each language).

2 If a language does not have negative concord, it is likely to have negative
polarity items, which are typically used only in negative clauses, questions,
and comparisons.

3 In many languages the scope of a negative is left-to-right; in at least a few,
such as English, it is more complex, and that too has to be learned.

Further Reading

English negation is dealt with comprehensively by Quirk et al. 1980: 374–85 (including
interesting observations on the interaction of scope and intonation in some
dialects). Butt and Benjamin 2011: 336–46 provide thorough discussion for
Spanish; Gildersleeve and Lodge 1895: 287–90, and especially Pinkster 2015, ch. 8,
do the same for Latin.

21 | Questions

How questions are handled also differs from language to language, but there are some fundamental similarities. There is a basic distinction between questions to which a yes-or-no-answer can be given and questions that include INTERROGATIVE pronouns, such as 'who?' and 'what?', or interrogative adverbs, like 'where?' and 'why?'. I treat them in that order.

In Navajo, a yes-or-no question is preceded by *da'*. There is no other change in the sentence:

Da' dichin ni'niiłhį́? 'Are you hungry?'

(Young and Morgan 1980, grammar p. 67)

Such questions can be answered with *'aoo'* 'yes' or *dooda* 'no'.

The Biblical Hebrew particle h^a-, prefixed to the first word in the sentence (either the verb or another constituent that has been moved to the beginning to be questioned), is exactly similar:

H^aṯimšōl bānū? 'Are you going to rule over us?'

The answer repeats the questioned word.

Mandarin likewise has a particle *ma* that marks yes-or-no questions. It appears at the end of the clause, and there is no other change:

Nǐ huì shuō Pǔtōnghuà ma? 你会说普通话吗? 'Are you able to speak Mandarin?'

The question is usually answered by repeating the (first) verb:

Bú huì. 不会. 'I can't.'

If the question is about a state, it is more idiomatic to answer with *shì de* 'yes' or *bú shì* 'no' (literally 'it isn't'):

Nǐ gǎnmào le ma? – Shì de. 你感冒了吗? – 是的.
'Have you got a cold?' – 'Yes.'

(Yip and Rimmington 1997: 104)

It is also common to pose a question by stating the alternatives:

Tā míngtiān lái   bù   lái? 她明天来不来? 'Is she coming tomorrow?'
(she tomorrow come [or] not come, p. 106)

In that case too the answer simply repeats the verb (positive or negative).

The Latin system is also fairly simple. The question particle is *–ne*. It is attached to the word being questioned (the verb, if no specific word is questioned), and that word tends to be placed at the beginning of the sentence, e.g.:

Omnisne pecūnia dissolūta est? 'Has all the money been spent?'
(Cicero, *Against Verres* III.77.180, quoted by Gildersleeve and Lodge 1895: 291)

If the speaker expects an affirmative answer, *nōnne* is instead placed at the beginning of the sentence; if a negative answer, *num* is used. If no question particle is used, the question is emphatic and emotional:

Īnfēlīx est Fabricius quod rūs suum fodit?! 'Fabricius is unhappy because he digs his own land?!'
(Seneca, *Dialogues* I.3.6, quoted ibid.)

A Latin question can be answered by repeating the verb, or the questioned word, but there are also words for 'yes' and 'no', as in English.

Like Mandarin, Latin has a construction for posing alternative questions, but it is used much less often:

Vōsne Lūcium Domitium an vōs Domitius dēseruit? 'Have you (pl.) deserted Lucius Domitius, or has Domitius deserted you?'

(Caesar, *Civil War* II.32.8)

There are minor variations on the latter construction: see Gildersleeve and Lodge 1895: 293–94, from which the above quotation is taken.

Unlike its ancestor, Spanish has no particle to mark yes-and-no questions. Instead the subject is usually placed after the verb:[1]

¿Ha llamado mi hermano? 'Has my brother called?'

Notice that the subject is placed after the entire verb phrase, not just after the auxiliary. It can even be placed after the direct object:

¿Ha traído Miguel flores? / ¿Ha traído flores Miguel? 'Has Michael brought flowers?'

If either the subject or the direct object is significantly longer, the longer item is placed last:

¿Ha traído flores el vecino de tu suegra? 'Has your mother-in-law's neighbor brought flowers?'

¿Ha traído Miguel las flores que encargamos? 'Has Michael brought the flowers that we ordered?'

As in Latin, it is also possible to ask a question with no overt marking except intonation, e.g.:

¿Usted quiere venir conmigo? 'You want to come with me?'

But such questions don't seem to be particularly emphatic. Like English, Spanish has answer words for 'yes' (*sí*) and 'no' (*no*).

Like Spanish, English postposes the subject in yes-and-no questions, but it is placed immediately after the first auxiliary:

Is she coming tomorrow?
Has my brother called?
Will you be completely healed in a couple of weeks?

---

[1] The following examples are from Butt and Benjamin 2011: 523.

The same peculiarity that we encountered in the discussion of negatives reappears in questions: if there is no auxiliary, *do* must be inserted. Otherwise the usual rules are followed:

Does she know this person?

If the negative has been contracted with the auxiliary, the subject follows the whole contracted sequence:

Don't the legislators understand that rail transit is underfunded?

In fact, negative contraction is normal in these instances, at least in colloquial English. You can say

Do the legislators not understand ...

but the effect is somewhat more emphatic.

The most basic interrogative words are usually the interrogative pronouns. Because the distinction between people and just about everything else is so fundamental in human societies, it is common for languages to have a pronoun meaning 'who?' and another meaning 'what?'. That is exactly the situation in Biblical Hebrew:

Mī 'attā ūmā ze? 'Who are you and what is this?'

In the Hebrew examples that I have seen, the interrogative pronoun is usually placed first in the sentence, as in English. For instance, at the beginning of *Psalm* 27:

> YHWH   *'ōrī*   *wəyiš'ī;*   *mimmī*   *'īrā?*
> 'The Lord (is) my light and my salvation; of whom should I be afraid?'

the interrogative is placed first in the second clause even though it is the object of a preposition (literally 'from'), and the preposition is therefore fronted with it, exactly as in Latin or formal English.

Although Navajo uses a large number of interrogative words (Young and Morgan 1980, grammar pp. 67–72), and their syntax is not clearly explained in the literature, it is at least clear that there is a word meaning 'who?' as opposed to other interrogatives:

Háílá shilééchąą'í yik'élwod? 'Who found my dog?'

Díí ha'át'íí' át'é? 'What is this?'

Haalá / daalá yinílyé? 'What is your name?' (or, 'How are you named?')

As the second example shows, interrogatives are not necessarily fronted in Navajo.

Mandarin makes the same distinction between 'who?' and 'what?', but note the word order of the following sentences:

Tāmende lǎoshī shì shéi? 他们的老师是谁? 'Who is their teacher?'

Nǐ zhǎo shénme? 你找什么? 'What are you looking for?'

In English the interrogative pronoun is usually first, whether it is the subject of the clause (as in the first example) or not (as in the second). In Mandarin the interrogative pronoun occupies *whatever position the corresponding noun phrase will occupy in the answer*. In the first case the answer would be something like

Tāmende lǎoshī shì Lǐ xiānshēng. 他们的老师是李先生. 'Their teacher is Mr. Lee.'

so the interrogative pronoun is last in the clause; you can see that the reasoning in the second example is the same, since direct objects follow their verbs in Mandarin (see Lesson 6). The interrogative pronoun is first only if it corresponds to the subject in the answer, e.g.

Shéi náqù le wǒde bǐ? 谁拿去了我的笔? 'Who took my pen?'

There are other languages that shift the interrogative pronoun to the beginning of the sentence, and other languages that do not.

Most of the other interrogative expressions in Mandarin include *shénme*; for instance, 'when?' is *shénme shíhou* 什么时候 (literally 'what time?'), and 'why?' is *wèi shénme* 为什么 (literally 'what for?'). But 'where?' is usually *nǎr*, and 'which?' is *nǎ*, which must be followed by a classifier:

Qǐngwèn, cèsuǒ zài nǎr? 请问, 厕所在哪儿? 'Please, where is the rest room?'

Nǐ xǐhuan nǎ běn shū? 你喜欢哪本书. 'Which book do you like?'

As you might expect, possession by an interrogative pronoun is expressed straightforwardly in Mandarin:

Zhèi zhī qiānbǐ shì shéide? 这枝铅笔是谁的? 'Whose pencil is this?'

(Yip and Rimmington 1997: 23)

You might expect that each language handles possession by interrogatives like possession by other pronouns, and many do. However, both Hebrew and Navajo treat interrogative pronouns like nouns in expressing possession. Thus in Hebrew we find the construct state followed by 'who?', as if the latter were a noun, e.g. in *Genesis* 24.23:

Baṯ-mī   *'att?*   'Whose daughter are you?'
(daughter-who (are) you (fem.))

In Navajo *hái* is used with the 3rd-person possessive *bi-*, just as if it were a noun:

Díishą'   *hái*   *bichidí?*   'Whose car is this?'
(this   who   his-car)

(Young and Morgan 1980, dictionary p. 398)

Latin interrogative pronouns might be expected to have a full set of forms for gender, number, and case, like the 3rd-person pronoun. But although neuter *quid* is distinguished from non-neuter *quis* (in the nominative and accusative), masculine and feminine are not distinguished for 'who?', and there are no plural forms – so that the system resembles that of Mandarin much more than might be expected. That makes sense in real-world terms, since the gender and number of what is being asked about are typically not known. Possession is simply expressed by the genitive, as for other nominals. 'Which', which is an adjective, does have a full set of forms, as expected. Latin also has an extensive set of interrogative adjectives and adverbs: *quot* 'how many?', *quandō* 'when?', *ubi* 'where', *cūr* 'why?', etc. The interrogative word typically appears first in the sentence, but otherwise there is no change in word order.

The Spanish system resembles the Latin system from which it is descended, but there are a couple of differences. As in Latin, the interrogative word usually appears first; but the verb usually follows, and the subject follows the verb unless it is the interrogative word:

¿Cómo se   llama su amigo? 'What's your friend's name?'
(how himself calls your friend)
¿Cuándo pagará el reya sus sirvientes? 'When <u>will</u> the king <u>pay</u> his servants?'
¿Quién sabe la verdad? 'Who knows the truth?'

(The interrogative is the subject in the last sentence.) If there is a direct object and it is shorter than the subject, even the direct object precedes the subject, just as in yes-or-no questions:

¿Dónde compran pan los campesinos del pueblo? 'Where do the people of the village buy bread?'

Another complication is the use of *cuál*. In principle *cuál* means 'which one?', but it is used when other languages use *what* or its equivalent if a choice is even remotely possible, e.g.:

¿Cuál es la diferencia? 'What's the difference?'

The default word for 'what', *qué*, is used in asking general questions or questions about the nature of something, e.g.:

¿Qué hora es? 'What time is it?'
¿Qué es la vida humana? 'What is human life?'

Strangely enough, *qué* is used as an adjective meaning 'which' before a noun in many dialects of Spanish, e.g.:

¿Qué diputados están presentes? 'Which members of parliament are present?'

On the other hand, 'who' is always *quién*, and 'whose' is simply *de quién*, literally 'of whom':

¿De quién es esa tienda? 'Whose shop is this?'

(The inherited word for 'whose', *cuyo*, is now archaic and literary.)

Like Spanish, English places the subject after the verb in this kind of question unless the interrogative word is the subject, but of course only after the first auxiliary, as in yes-and-no questions:

Who knows the truth? (who is subject)
When will you be coming back?

If there is no auxiliary, the do-support rule applies:

Why did you run away?

Unlike Spanish, English has retained a bit of case-marking on its interrogative pronouns: *whom* is the objective form of *who*, and there is a possessive adjective *whose.* However, the objective caseform is being lost. Although in formal English one says

> *Whom did you see?*

because *whom* is the direct object of *see*, in colloquial English

> *Who did you see?*

is now much more normal. But so far the loss is limited. If you move an interrogative out of a prepositional phrase, stranding the preposition, it's normal to drop the objective form:

> <u>Who</u> *did you give it <u>to</u>?*

But if you move the preposition with it, the objective form is retained:

> *<u>To whom</u> did you give it? / *To who did you give it?*

Of course that might be connected with the fact that fronting the preposition with its interrogative object is a somewhat more formal construction.

This last point brings up a further peculiarity of English, namely preposition STRANDING. There is nothing like it in Latin or Spanish (or Italian, or French, or German, or Hebrew …). In most languages that front interrogatives you must front the preposition with its interrogative object, e.g.:

> *¿A quién lo dio usted?* 'To whom did you give it?' / '<u>Who</u> did you give it <u>to</u>?'
> *Quā dē causā hoc fēcistī?* 'For what <u>reason</u> did you do this?' / '<u>What</u> did you do this <u>for</u>?'

Some teachers condemn preposition stranding in the belief that it's "bad grammar," but in fact the construction is very old: I recall finding an example in *Sir Gawain and the Green Knight*, a famous narrative poem written around 1400. It's good, traditional native English; it just happens to be different from Latin, for example. (On the concept of "bad grammar," see the Epilogue.)

Further Reading

On English questions see Gelderen 2002: 181–82 and especially Quirk et al. 1980: 387–402; for Spanish, Butt and Benjamin 2011: 347–53; for Latin, Gildersleeve and Lodge 1895: 290–9; for Mandarin, Yip and Rimmington 1997: 99–108. Pinkster 2015, ch. 6, is broader, discussing all Latin types of main clause.

22 | Adjectives and Relative Clauses

Languages often have alternative ways of saying the same thing. We have seen that word order is flexible in Latin, that an active sentence can be recast as passive in many languages, that the indirect object of 'give' can be expressed in two different ways in English (though not in our other languages), and so on. This lesson will discuss a pair of alternative structures that recur in a large majority of languages.

English routinely embeds adjectives in noun phrases (see Lessons 4 and 8); if more than one adjective is used, their order tends to be fixed, e.g.:

the *little old red* wagon (but not **the red old little wagon*; maybe ?*the old little red wagon*, if you're talking about little red wagons and there's more than one)

All the adjectives follow the definite article *the* and precede the noun.[1] However, there is an alternative; you can say

the little old wagon *which is red*

---

[1] None of the statements about adjectives in this lesson necessarily apply to adjectives that are more "grammatical": possessive adjectives (which are treated in Lesson 11), quantifiers like 'all', determiners like 'this' and 'that'. In this lesson I discuss only those adjectives that have fully "lexical" meanings.

(e.g. if there's more than one wagon and only one is red). The clause *which is red* is called a RELATIVE CLAUSE; relative clauses are clauses that are embedded in noun phrases, just like adjectives, and (as you can see) they can convey the same information as adjectives. In English they follow the noun rather than precede it.

But because they are more complex, relative clauses can also convey much more information than an adjective, or than any single word. Typical English examples are:

> the kind of tea *that he prefers*
> the guest *who arrived last night*
> the applicant *whose file I haven't seen yet*

English has several different relative pronouns: *that, which*, and the paradigm *who, whom, whose* (but not *what*) are all used to introduce relative clauses in standard English (though they all also have other uses). It is also possible to omit the relative pronoun in English:

> the man *I saw* = the man *that I saw*;

so that only word order indicates that a relative clause is being used; that is not possible in our other languages. There are also relative adverbs, e.g.:

> This is the place *where* it all falls apart.
> I don't remember a time *when* I didn't know that.
> Give me a good reason *why* I should do that.

Like all clauses, relative clauses are unbounded, both in variety and in length; they can get too long to understand or remember, but there is no grammatical limit.

Spanish and Latin adjectives and relative clauses resemble those of English, although there are some differences of detail. Spanish adjectives agree with their nouns in gender and number; Latin adjectives agree with their nouns in gender, number, and case (see Lessons 8 and 12). In neither language do adjectives occupy fixed positions in the noun phrase the way they do in English. Spanish adjectives normally follow their nouns if they are RESTRICTIVE, i.e. if they narrow down the referent of the noun phrase, e.g.:

> *el español americano* 'American Spanish'
> *una camisa limpia* 'a clean shirt'

Otherwise they can precede or follow the noun; more often they follow, and the rules for when they precede are complex and not without exceptions (see Butt and Benjamin 2011: 61–70). In Latin, the position of adjectives is even more variable. In both languages there is a tendency to place the adjective before the noun if it is emphatic.

Both in Spanish and in Latin, relative clauses typically follow the noun, as in English. Spanish uses a variety of relative pronouns, just as English does: *quien* 'who' (pl. *quienes*), *que* 'that', and *cual* 'which' (pl. *cuales*); but *cual* is usually preceded by the definite article, and sometimes *que* is too. Latin has a single relative pronoun *quī*, with a complete set of forms for gender, number, and case, which is identical with the interrogative adjective meaning 'which'. Both Spanish and Latin also have relative adverbs much like those of English.

Hebrew adjectives behave very much like Spanish adjectives, agreeing in gender and number with the nouns that head their noun phrases:

'īš ḥāḵām 'wise man'	*bayit gāḏōl*	'big house'	(masc. sg.)
'iššā ḥəzāqā 'strong woman'	*'īr gəḏōlā*	'large city'	(fem. sg.)
dəḇārīm ṭōḇīm 'good words'	*'āḇōṯ zəqēnīm*	'old fathers'	(masc. pl.)
ḥayyōṯ rā'ōṯ 'evil beasts'	*'ittīm šəlēmōṯ*	'complete seasons'	(fem. pl.)

In Hebrew the adjective follows its head noun, and (as in Spanish and Latin), although the gender and number must agree, the endings can be different (as in several examples adduced here).

Hebrew relative clauses, however, are somewhat different from those of the European languages. There is a relative particle *'ašer* that typically introduces the clause. If the head noun of the noun phrase is the subject or direct object of the relative clause, the particle effectively does duty as a relative pronoun, e.g.:

'*Ašrē hā'īš 'ašer lō hālaḵ …*
(happy the-man REL not walk-PERF-3SGMASC)
'Happy (is) the man who does not walk …'

(*Psalms* 1.1)

… haddəḇārīm hā'ēlle 'ašer 'ānōḵī məṣawwəḵā …
(the-words the-these REL I commanding-you)
'… these things which I am enjoining on you …'

(*Deuteronomy* 6.6)

But if the head noun has some other function in the relative clause, it must be repeated by a pronoun or adverb, e.g.:

'īš "ᵃšer Mṓše šǝmṓ
(man REL Moses name-his)
'a man that his name (was) Moses', i.e. 'a man whose name was Moses'
'ereṣ "ᵃšer leḥem šām
(land REL bread there)
'a land that (there is) bread there', i.e. 'a land where there is food'

This resembles Old English relative constructions, although the details are different.

Mandarin adjectives and relative clauses constitute a single system which is quite different from those of the languages just discussed.[2] Everything in the system is placed after the classifier (if there is one; see Lesson 12) but before the noun. A single monosyllabic adjective precedes the noun with no linking particle, e.g.:

hǎo péngyou 好朋友 'good friends'
yì tiáo hóng qúnzi 一条红裙 'a red skirt'
xīn yīfu 新衣服 'new clothes'

A few disyllabic adjectives and phrases behave the same way, e.g.:

cǎisè diànshi 彩色电视 'color television'
hěn duō rén 很多人 'lots of people'
(very many people)
bù shǎo shū 不少书 'a considerable number of books'
(not few book)

But most modifiers longer than a single syllable – including most phrases that include the adverb hěn 'very' – must be followed by the particle de 的, e.g.:

piàoliàng de yīfu 票亮的衣服 'beautiful clothes'
hěn xīn de yīfu 很新的衣服 'brand-new clothes'

This is the same particle that is used to indicate possession (see Lesson 11). Relative clauses are handled in exactly the same way: the entire clause is followed by de, which is followed by the noun. The following examples are typical:

---

[2] The examples in this paragraph are from Yip and Rimmington 1997: 25–28.

mài bàozhǐ de shāngdiàn 买报纸的商店 'a shop that <u>sells newspapers</u>'
yào xǐ de yīfu 要洗的衣服 'clothes that <u>need washing</u>'
nǐ yào fù de qián 你要付的钱 'the money that <u>you must pay</u>'

There is no relative pronoun; the relationship between the noun and the relative clause is inferred from context. This is a striking example of units with the same syntactic function – adjectives, possessives, and relative clauses, all modifying nouns within a noun phrase – being handled by the same grammatical machinery.

As I observed in Lesson 8, Navajo does not have any adjectives, only stative verbs meaning 'be X' (where X would be expressed by an adjective in many other languages). It does have relative clauses, however, and an English adjective is usually translatable by a relative clause containing a stative verb. For instance (cf. Young and Morgan 1980, grammar p. 56):

Ké łizhin. 'The shoes are black.'
ké łizhinígíí 'shoes which are black', 'black shoes'

As you can see, the relative clause is marked by a suffix *-ígíí* on the verb and follows the head noun. Other relative clauses are constructed in exactly the same way (examples from Young and Morgan 1980, grammar p. 56):

Hastiin bináá'   *dootł'izh.*   'The man's eyes are blue.'
(man   his-eyes   be-blue)
hastiin bináá' dootł'izhígíí 'the man whose eyes are blue', 'the blue-eyed man'

she'esdzáán   *'éétsoh*   *shá*   *'áyiilaaígíí*
(my-wife   coat   me-for   make-3sg-PERF-REL)[3]
'the coat (that) my wife made for me'

The last example shows that in some cases the head noun can be inside the relative clause; we do not need to discuss that complication here (although it does recur in Latin). Otherwise Navajo *-ígíí* is very much like Mandarin *de*: it simply marks the clause as relative, leaving the hearer to figure out from context what the exact relation between the head noun and the relative clause is.

---

[3] *-yi-* 3sg. object, *-i-* perfective; the 3sg. subject is unmarked.

To Be Remembered from Lesson 22

Adjectives within noun phrases and relative clauses perform the same basic function – modifying the head noun of the noun phrase – so that an adjective can usually be replaced by a relative clause, and languages that have relative clauses (i.e. most languages) do not strictly need adjectives.

Further Reading

On English relative clauses see Gelderen 2002: 168–74 and Quirk et al. 1980: 860–74; on Spanish, Butt and Benjamin 2011: 502–12; on Latin, Gildersleeve and Lodge 1895: 393–408.

23 | Articles, Demonstratives, and Quantifiers

The last lesson discussed some different types of qualifier that can be part of noun phrases. There are several other types of functional marker that also occur in noun phrases; they are the subject of this lesson.

ARTICLES are function words that indicate whether a noun phrase is DEFINITE or INDEFINITE. English and Spanish have similar systems: the English definite article *the* corresponds fairly closely to Spanish *el, la*, plural *los, las* (and *lo* to introduce "headless" relative clauses: *lo que* '. . . that which . . .'), while the English indefinite article *a* (*an* before vowels) corresponds fairly closely to Spanish *un, una* – and in both languages the article precedes the noun-plus-adjective complex (*the good pope*; *el papa bueno*). In general, the definite article indicates that the noun phrase refers to a specific entity (*the politician that you know*; *el político cual usted conoce*), while the indefinite article indicates that the noun phrase refers to any of a class of entities (*a politician*; *un político*). English has no plural indefinite article, although *some* can be used to supply it; Spanish has plural *unos, unas* (*(some) politicians*; *unos políticos*). There are various idiosyncracies of detail; for instance, in English we make generic statements like *man is a rational animal* or *people are stupid*, while Spanish uses the definite article but not the indefinite: *el hombre es animal racional*; *los hombres son tontos*. But the main systematic difference is that Spanish articles must agree in gender and number with their nouns, while English has no such agreement (anywhere in the grammar).

Biblical Hebrew has a definite article, which is *ha-*, *hā-*, or (occasionally) *he-* depending on what follows, but no indefinite article. Thus *hā'iššā* is 'the woman', while *'iššā* is 'woman' or 'a woman'; *hannāšīm* is 'the women', while *nāšīm* is 'women' or 'some women'.

Latin has no articles at all; whether a noun phrase is definite or indefinite must be deduced from context. Strictly speaking, Navajo and Mandarin also have no articles. For example:

E		S		H		L		N		M
the dog	=	*el perro*	=	*hakkeleƀ*	=	*canis*	=	*łééchąą'í*	=	*gǒu*
a dog	=	*un perro*	=	*keleƀ*	=	*canis*	=	*łééchąą'í*	=	*gǒu*
the dogs	=	*los perros*	=	*hakkəlāƀīm*	=	*canēs*	=	*łééchąą'í*	=	*gǒu*
(some) dogs	=	*unos perros*	=	*kəlāƀīm*	=	*canēs*	=	*łééchąą'í*	=	*gǒu*

In Navajo and Mandarin even the number of the noun has to be inferred, as we saw in Lesson 4.

However, Mandarin has begun to develop a way of signalling the difference between definite and indefinite noun phrases, and Navajo might be doing likewise. In Mandarin, *yī* 'one' can sometimes be used as an indefinite article, e.g.:

> *yi*[1] *ge shífēn   zhòng de bāoguǒ*   一个十分重的包裹
> (one CL ten-point heavy PTCL package)
> 'an extremely heavy package' (Yip and Rimmington 1997: 25)

It also occurs in two fixed phrases involving classifiers, in which it corresponds closely to English *a*:

> *yi xiē shū* 一些书 'a few books; some books'
> *yi diǎnr yán* 一点儿盐 'a little salt'

---

[1] The tones of this word exhibit a phenomenon called tone sandhi. In isolation the word is *yī*, but at the beginning of a noun phrase it appears as *yi*. However, if the next word also has a falling tone, *yi* becomes *yí*, with a rising tone. In this sentence the next word, the classifier *gè*, has a falling tone underlyingly, which causes the shift to *yí*; on the surface, however, *ge* has been destressed and has therefore lost its tone. This is all merely phonology, i.e. rules of pronunciation; it has nothing to do with meaning.

Mandarin does not yet have an obligatory indefinite article, but it looks like one might be developing. Interestingly, the Spanish indefinite article is also obviously a form of 'one', and English *a, an* was originally a destressed form of 'one'; evidently that numeral is a usual historical source of indefinite articles.

The Navajo situation is harder to assess. The relative particle *-ígíí* (see the preceding lesson) can also be affixed to nouns, and it serves to single them out. For instance, it seems that if you say

> *Ch'ahígíí bił   yóó' 'ííyol.*   'The wind blew the hat away.'
> (hat-REL it-with away blow-PERF)

you imply that the hat (*ch'ah*) is the only thing that was blown away (Young and Morgan 1980, grammar p. 57); in fact, this sentence might equally well be translated as 'It was the hat that the wind blew away.' The grammatical status of *-ígíí* in cases like this is not clear to me, although its function seems to overlap with that of a definite article.

DEMONSTRATIVES are more specific than definite articles; they indicate a definite referent *and* locate it relative to the person speaking and/or the person spoken to. In many languages they occupy the same position in the noun phrase as the definite article, but in others they occur with the article. English, Hebrew, and Mandarin have a simple two-member system of demonstratives that is very widespread among the world's languages: English *this* (pl. *these*), Hebrew *ze* (fem. *zōt*, pl. *'ēlle*), and Mandarin *zhèi* indicate a referent relatively close to the speaker, while English *that* (pl. *those*), Hebrew *hū* (fem. *hī*, pl. masc. *hēmmā*, fem. *hēnnā*), and Mandarin *nèi* indicate one farther away. For instance:

M	E	H
zhèi běn shū =	*this book / these books* =	*hassēper hazze / hassəpārīm hā'ēlle*
nèi běn shū =	*that book / those books* =	*hassēper hāhū / hassəpārīm*
		hāhēmmā

Note that, whereas in Mandarin and English the demonstratives come first in the noun phrase, so that in English they occupy the same place as the article and in Mandarin the same place where *yì* 'one / a(n)' would appear, in Hebrew the structure is different: the noun is preceded by the definite article; the demonstrative follows and is also preceded by the definite article.

Spanish and Latin have three-member demonstrative systems, and such systems are also fairly common crosslinguistically. However, their systems are not identical. Spanish *este, esta* (pl. *estos, estas*) corresponds closely to English *this* (pl. *these*) and Mandarin *zhèi*; so does Latin *hic*, which (like the other demonstratives) has a full set of forms for gender, number, and case. Otherwise the systems diverge. Spanish *ese, esa* (pl. *esos, esas*) corresponds to English *that* (pl. *those*) and Mandarin *nèi*; but Spanish has a further option, *aquel, aquella* (pl. *aquellos, aquellas*) meaning 'that (way over there)' or 'that (remote in time)' when the speaker wishes to emphasize distance:[2]

> ¿Como se llama aquella estrella? 'What is that star called?' (but *esa estrella* is also acceptable)
> *no esa torre sino aquella* 'not that tower but *that* one (further off)'

Latin divides up 'that' differently. The usual word is *ille*; the alternative *iste* indicates something close to or associated with the person spoken to, e.g.:[3]

> *Adventū tuō ista subsellia vacuēfacta sunt.* 'At your arrival the benches near you emptied out.'
> (Cicero, *Against Catiline* I.7.16, quoted by Gildersleeve and Lodge 1895: 192)

Navajo makes many more distinctions among its demonstratives, to judge from Young and Morgan 1980, grammar pp. 28–29, dictionary pp. 340–41, 362, 525–26, 677. Both *díí* and its extended form *díidí* correspond to English 'this'; they apparently contrast with *'eii* and *'eiidí*, which are translated as 'that' but refer to something relatively close to the speaker and visible. *Naghái* refers to something further off, often near the person addressed (like Latin *iste*); *ńléí* and *ńlááh* refer to something in the distance, but still visible. Finally, *'éí* and *'éidí* refer to something remote and invisible.

Unlike articles, demonstratives can be whole noun phrases themselves, e.g.:

---

[2] These examples are from Butt and Benjamin 2011: 83–85.

[3] The Latin and Spanish forms obviously resemble one another, but you can see that their functions have shifted during the development of Latin into Spanish. Latin *ille* 'that' is the source of the Spanish article *el* (and the 3rd-person pronoun *él*); it is also the second part of *aquel*, which was originally a compound. Latin *iste* 'that (of yours)' is the source of Spanish *este* 'this'. Spanish *ese* 'that' is descended from the Latin emphatic pronoun *ipse* 'the very same, he himself'; Latin *hic* has been lost in Spanish (and most other Romance languages).

E   *What is this / that?*
S   *¿Qué es esto / eso?*
L   *Quid hoc / illud?*   (what (is) this / that)
H   *Ma-zze? / Mā hū?*   (what (is) this / that)
N   *Díí / ’eii ha’át’íí ’át’é?*   (this / that what is)
M   *Zhè / nà shi shénme?*   (this / that is what)

In these sentences Spanish uses the form that does not agree with any noun; Latin can omit the verb 'is', and Hebrew always does; Mandarin uses forms slightly different from the ones used with nouns. But those are all incidental details that don't affect the point under discussion.

Finally, noun phrases can include QUANTIFIERS, which indicate number and amount, precisely or vaguely. Numerals are quantifiers; in many languages some have idiosyncratic inflectional forms, and some behave like nouns: for instance, Latin *centum*, Spanish *ciento*, and Hebrew *mē’āh* 'hundred' are nouns, although in English, Navajo, and Mandarin 'hundred' behaves like other numerals (i.e. like a demonstrative). But the interesting quantifiers are the more general ones, such as 'all' and 'some', which will be discussed briefly here.

What is unusual about *all* in English is its position. Unlike other components of the noun phrase, it precedes a definite article or demonstrative:

all the world
all those larger units

(but *the whole world*; *those three larger units*). It can also "float" within its clause. For instance, you can say

Not all the guests have come.

or you can say

The guests haven't all come.

and they mean the same thing. *Some* and *none* (or *no*) don't have those properties. We say:

Some / no guests have come.
Some / none of the guests have come.

But we can also say

All of the guests have come.

The system is complicated, with some alternatives but more constraints, and is therefore difficult to learn.

One peculiarity of the English system recurs in Spanish: Spanish *todo* 'all' precedes an article in the noun phrase. Thus in Spanish we find

todo el mundo   'all the world / the whole world'
todos los mayores   'all the larger ones'

(but *los tres mayores* 'the three larger ones'). So far as I can discover, *todo* does not float in the way English *all* does. You can postpose it to the end of a sentence, e.g.:

Somos cansados todos.

but in that case it indicates heavy emphasis: 'We are *all* tired.'

Hebrew *kol-* 'all' likewise precedes the article in a noun phrase but has no other peculiarities, e.g.:

kol-hā'āreṣ   'all the earth'
kol-šōp̄əṭē-Yiśrā'ēl   'all the judges of Israel'

Mandarin, by contrast, takes the "dislocation" of 'all' one step further than English. There is an adjective *suŏyŏu* that means 'all' and is used just like any other adjective:

suŏyŏu de fángzi 'all the houses'

But the most common way of expressing 'all' is an adverb *dōu* which immediately precedes the verb but modifies the first noun phrase in the sentence (either the subject or a topic that has been fronted), much like English floated *all*, e.g.:[4]

Tāmen dōu qù chī wŭfàn le. 'They have all gone to lunch'
Nèi ge diànyĭng wŏ dōu xĭhuan. 'I like all those films.'

---

[4] These examples are adapted from Yip and Rimmington 1997: 81–82.

At the other end of the spectrum there is nothing special about the syntax of Latin *omnis* 'all': it's just an adjective that happens to have a quantifying function.[5]

In Navajo 'all' seems to be expressed by phrases including the verb 'be' or a verb meaning 'be large, be many', e.g.:

> *t'áá 'ániit'é* 'all of us'   *t'áá 'át'éé n̓t'éé'* 'all of it/them, entirely'
> *t'áá 'ánóht'é* 'all of you'

As you must have guessed by now, this discussion of quantifiers barely scratches the surface. The syntax of quantifiers (in some languages, at least) is as complex as the syntax of negation, and for the same reason: this is an area where natural human language intersects with formal logic, and the two are very different.

Exercise

Consider the following sentences in Old English, in which articles and demonstratives have been underlined. Note that the difference between *sē* and *sēo* is one of gender (masculine vs. feminine). What was unusual about the articles and demonstratives of Old English?

> *Þēs wela is eorðlić, ac sē wela is heofonlić.* 'This happiness is mundane, but that happiness is celestial.'
> *Sē dǣġ eallum hālgum ġehālgod is; þēs dǣġ is ealra daga hālgost.* 'That day is dedicated to all saints; this day is (the) holiest of all days.'
> *Þēs hāliġ wer Stephanus wearþ sē forma cȳðere.* 'This holy man Stephen became the first martyr.'
> *Nū is ūre wiðerwinna þēs wælhrēowa heretoga; ōðer is sē dēma, and sē dēofol þridda.* 'Now this bloodthirsty commander is our adversary; a second is the judge, and the devil (is the) third.'

---

[5] *Omnis* appears often after the noun that it qualifies, but that is because nouns qualified by *omnis* are often raised out of their noun phrases for emphasis; see Devine and Stephens 2006: 507–11 for discussion.

Sum mann sēow gōd sǣd on his æcere; þā cōm his fēonda sum and ofersēow hit mid coccele. Þā sēo wyrt wēox, þā ætīewde sē coccel hine. 'A man sowed good seed in his field; then one of his enemies came and re-sowed it with weeds. When the crop grew, the weeds showed themselves.'

Further Reading

Gelderen 2002 briefly discusses the structure of noun phrases on pp. 151–54; Quirk et al. 1980 have more extensive discussion on pp. 147–65 and 902–34. Discussion of corresponding phenomena in the other languages can be found in the standard grammars.

24 Subordinate Clauses, Infinitives, and Verbal Nouns

Languages need to be able to make complex statements in which one part is subordinated to another. At least the following relations need to be expressed (I give English examples for each):

1) Objects of verbs of knowing, saying, wanting, etc., e.g.:
   I know that he left on Tuesday.
   John said that he wasn't going to be there.
   I want to go to Canada this summer.
   I intend to finish as soon as possible.
2) Indirect questions depending on verbs of knowing and saying, e.g.:
   I don't know whether or not he'll show up.
   I don't know what to do.
   He wouldn't say how he was going to vote.
3) Statements of causation, e.g.:
   The bolt won't fit because it's too thick.
4) Statements of intention and the like without a specific governing verb, e.g.:
   I'm going home to get some rest.
   One has to have a good deal of luck in order to succeed.

5) Statements of temporal relationship, e.g.:

When he can't find it he'll just give up.

Whenever I try to figure it out I get a headache.

After I run a few errands I'll eat lunch.

While they were looking at it a whole chunk of the glacier slid into the water.

6) Statements of condition, including unexpected failure of condition, e.g.:

If I discover something really interesting I'll let you know.

If I knew what to do I'd tell you.

Although he's been wrong plenty of times before his confidence is unimpaired.

The underlined clauses are SUBORDINATE CLAUSES: they cannot constitute full sentences on their own (whereas most of the main clauses, like *he'll just give up*, can). In addition, verbs of fearing, permitting, hindering, etc. govern special types of subordinate clauses in some languages.

In most languages most of these relationships are expressed by SUBORDINATING CONJUNCTIONS, such as English *that, whether, because, when, while, if, although*, etc. in the example sentences above. There is no need to rehearse them all here. Instead I will point out some of the ways in which languages' handling of subordinate clauses is idiosyncratic.

In several of the English sentences above, the subordinate clause has no expressed subject and the verb is introduced by the preposition *to*. That is how English marks INFINITIVES. One of the most important uses of infinitives is to express the objects of verbs like *want*; another is to express purpose, as in

I'm going home to get some rest.

Infinitives are also widely used in Spanish and Latin, and to some extent also in Hebrew, but they are not always used in the same constructions as in English. There are some close parallels, e.g. the use of an infinitive after 'be able':

E   *We are not able to say anything good or bad to you.*

S   *No le podemos decir a usted ni bueno ni malo.*

L   *Neu bonum neu malum tibī dīcere possumus.*

H   *Lō nōkal dabber 'ēlekā ra' 'ō-ṭōb.*

(*Genesis* 24.50)

Note that the infinitive is not preceded by any preposition or particle in the languages other than English; in those languages its inflection alone marks it as an infinitive. Both Spanish and Hebrew can also use the infinitive to indicate purpose, but in that case it must be preceded by a preposition:

E   *And he came down to see the city.*

S   *Bajó para ver la ciudad. (para* 'for')

H   *Wayyāreḏ lir'ōṯ 'eṯ-hā'îr.*

(*Genesis* 11.5; *li-* 'to')

Latin, however, does not use infinitives to express purpose. One must use another type of subordinate clause:

L   *Et   dēscendit   ut   urbem   vidēret.*
(and descend-PERF-3SG so-that city-ACC see-IMPF-SUBJ-3SG)

On the other hand, Latin routinely uses infinitives for the objects of verbs of saying and knowing, whereas our other languages use other types of clause. For instance:

E   *I know that he went down there.*

S   *Sé que bajó para allá.*

H   *Yāḏa'tî kî yāraḏ šāmmā.*

But, with an infinitive:

L   *Eum illūc   dēscendisse   sciō.*
(him to-there descend-PERF-INF know-1SG)

It is not quite impossible to say "I know him to have gone down there" in English, but it sounds so archaic as to be almost ridiculous; even "I know him to be a fool" is decidedly formal.

Neither Mandarin nor Navajo has infinitives.

In addition to its infinitive and the present participle in *-ing* (which we encountered in Lesson 14 and will meet again in Lesson 25), English has a verbal noun in *-ing* (sometimes called a "gerund" in traditional descriptions of English grammar). It can take the place of the infinitive when governed by some verbs. For instance,

I like reading.

is an exact equivalent of

I like to read.

However, the two are not always interchangeable;

I want to eat now.

is perfectly normal, whereas

*I want eating now.

is very strange, if not downright ungrammatical. Like the infinitive, the English verbal noun can govern a direct object, for instance:

Banning <u>newspapers</u> is a typical act of tyranny.

Moreover, although it is not passive, the English verbal noun can be accompanied by an agent phrase:

No amount of investigating <u>by corrupt politicians</u> will bring the truth to light.

Nevertheless the verbal noun is a noun; in the last example it is part of a prepositional phrase introduced by *of*, while in the preceding example it is the subject of *is*. Since it is clearly the direct object in the sentence *I like reading*, it follows that the infinitive is the direct object in *I like to read*. The dual function of these forms – nouns in relation to the main clause, but verbs in the abbreviated subordinate clauses that they form – adds a great deal of flexibility to the grammar of the language.

Hebrew also uses its verbal noun as an equivalent of a subordinate clause. An example is *II Kings* 19.1:

Wayhī   kišəmōᵃʻ hammelek Ḥizqiyyāhū, wayyiqəraʻ 'eṯ-bəḡāḏāw ...
(and-it-was as-<u>hearing</u> of-the-king Hezekiah,   and-he-tore PTCL-his-clothes ...)
'Now when King Hezekiah heard (this), he rent his garments ...'

The construction is somewhat different from those we have seen so far: the verbal noun is in the construct state (see Lesson 11), and its logical subject follows it in the normal position for a possessor. In other words, the syntax is entirely that of noun phrases, even though the meaning is that of a verb. We do not use the English verbal noun that way, but we do use other nouns derived from verbs in similar ways. For instance, in

> *the Romans' destruction of the city*

both the logical subject and the logical object of *destroy* are expressed formally as possessives, while in

> *the city's destruction by the Romans*

the logical object is expressed by a possessive phrase, while the logical subject is expressed by an agent phrase.

The most important conclusion from the above discussion is that infinitives and verbal nouns, and in some languages other nouns derived from verbs, can serve as slightly condensed subordinate clauses, but that where and how they're used is subject to the specific rules of each language, which must be learned individually.

Another complication involving subordinate clauses is that in European languages the tense of a subordinate clause often depends partly on the tense of the main clause; in addition, some languages, including Spanish and Latin, use the subjunctive mood in some kinds of subordinate clause.

In some cases a subjunctive has a definable meaning or function. We have already seen some Spanish examples in Lesson 15; here are a few more from Latin and Spanish. For instance, Latin conditional sentences make a three-way distinction:

> *Sī crēdis quae dīcunt, stultus es.* 'If you believe what they say, you're stupid.'
> *Sī crēdās quae dīcunt, stultus sīs.* 'If you were to believe what they say, you'd be stupid.'
> *Sī crēderēs quae dīcunt, stultus essēs.* 'If you believed what they say, you'd be stupid.'

The first sentence uses the present indicative in both clauses; it is completely straightforward, and that is reflected in the English translation. The second sentence uses the present subjunctive in both clauses, while the third uses the imperfect subjunctive in both, and they are less direct than the first sentence. The difference between them is that the third sentence assumes that you do *not* believe what they say, while the second leaves open the possibility that you might. Spanish, Latin's direct descendant, has simplified this system: the present subjunctive no longer occurs in conditional sentences, so that the difference of nuance between the second and third Latin types has been lost:

> Si crees lo que dicen, eres tonto. 'If you believe what they say, you're stupid.'
> Si creyeras lo que dicen, serías tonto. 'If you believed what they say, you'd be stupid.'

The first sentence has the present indicative in both clauses, like its Latin ancestor and its English translation. The second has the past subjunctive in the *if*-clause and the conditional in the main clause; it is more like its English translation than it is like its Latin ancestor(s).

In other cases, however, the subjunctive must be used because of a rule of grammar, and its function is less easy to define. For instance, a Latin clause that indicates the circumstances under which a past event happened normally uses the imperfect subjunctive introduced by *cum*, e.g.:

> Cum domum redīrem amīcō obviam iī.   'As I was returning home I ran into a friend.'

In most other circumstances, however, *cum* means 'when' and is followed by a verb in the indicative. For instance, in the similar sentence in Lesson 16:

> Domum redībam cum Mārcō obviam iī.   'I was returning home when I met Marcus.'

my returning home is presented as the main event, reported in the imperfect indicative, and running into Marcus is represented as a subsequent event, also in the indicative, even though it is a past event and the clause is introduced by *cum*. This is a very subtle distinction.

As with the use of infinitives, the use of subjunctives must be learned in detail for each language that has them.

A final point is that, while many languages have a wide array of subordinating conjunctions to express precise meaning relationships between the clauses, some do not: a language can get by with very few subordinators, relying on the hearer to deduce the logical relationship between the clauses from the context. Hebrew has famously few conjunctions of any kind. The only common subordinating conjunctions are *kī* 'that, because, when' and *'im-* 'if'; the relative particle *'ᵃšer* (see Lesson 22) is also used with prepositions to introduce subordinate clauses, e.g. *ka'ᵃšer* 'according to what' = 'as'.

To Be Remembered from Lesson 24

1. Infinitives are typically used as slightly condensed subordinate clauses; their use varies considerably among the languages that have them.
2. Subordinate clauses can be usefully classified partly in grammatical terms (e.g. objects of certain kinds of verb) and partly by function (temporal, conditional, etc.).
3. Rules governing the use of verb forms in subordinate clauses are often complex and idiosyncratic; conditional sentences are often among the most complexly rule-governed.

Further Reading

The topics covered in this lesson are so various that discussion is scattered across the standard grammars of each language.

25 | Participles

PARTICIPLES are the most versatile grammatical category. They are always made from verbs. We have seen them used with auxiliary verbs to create complex verb phrases (see Lessons 14 through 16); in that function they are simply forms of the verb, and the Hebrew use of active particples to express continuous action (see Lesson 17) is also purely verbal.

But participles are also adjectives that are regularly and productively derived from verbs. For instance, in English we say not only

They've <u>broken</u> the lock.

but also

The lock is <u>broken</u>. (i.e. in a broken state, not being broken right now)
the <u>broken</u> lock

using the past passive participle as an adjective. The present participle in *-ing* can be used the same way; we say not only

That contraption is <u>flying</u>.

but also

He wants a <u>flying</u> camel for his birthday.

Participles are like relative clauses condensed into a single word; *the broken lock* is equivalent to *the lock which has been broken*, *a flying camel* is equivalent to *a camel which flies*, and so on. For that reason they can take objects and in fact be the verb of a whole clause, e.g:

> They caught him *taking bribes from contractors.*

which means, in effect, *they observed him while he was taking. . .*

Spanish participles resemble English ones, but with an important difference. The uses of the past passive participle are almost exactly like those of English. For instance, the sentences and phrase using *broken* above can be translated into Spanish as

> *Han roto la cerradura.*
> *La cerradura está rota.*
> *una cerradura rota*

But present participles are a different story. The gerund in *-ndo*, which is used to form continuous tenses (such as *está lloviendo* 'it's raining (right now)'), cannot be used as an adjective. It is used together with a tensed verb to indicate simultaneous action and other similar relations (Butt and Benjamin 2011: 310–17). A typical example is

> *Entré en el cuarto gritando.* 'I entered the room (while) shouting.'

and we have seen that English uses its present participle in the same way. But if you want to say something like 'a flying camel', you have to say

> *un camello volante*;

such an adjectival participle in *-nte* is never used to make compound tenses, and in fact many verbs do not even have such a form. Unlike English participles, these adjectives can be used as nouns: it is normal to use *amante* for 'lover', *estudiante* for 'student', and so on.

Hebrew participles also resemble those of English; but except for the verbal use of the active participle noted above, they are clearly adjectives, and (like the Spanish participles in *-ante*) they can be used as nouns. However, the active participles of transitive verbs can take objects. For instance:

Bārū̱k 'attā, 'aḏōnāy, mele̱k hā'ōlām. 'Blessed (are) you, O Lord, king of the universe.' (passive participle)

... *kī hū nō̱tēn lə̱kā kō^aḥ la^{'a}śō̱t ḥāyil* '... for it is he who gives you power to acquire wealth' (active participle, *Deuteronomy* 8.18)[1]

... *wəšā̱ka̱htā 'e̱t-YHWH ^{'e}lōhe̱kā hammō̱ṣī'^{'a}̱kā mē'ereṣ miṣrayim* '... and you have forgotten the Lord your God who brought you out of the land of Egypt' (participle *mō̱ṣī'* 'causing to go out' with object *-kā* 'you')

The second and third examples show that a participle can perform the same function as a relative clause (which by now should not surprise you).

Latin has more participles than the languages discussed above: in addition to the familiar present active participle and perfect passive participle, there are two future participles, one active and one passive. All can be used as adjectives, e.g.:

currus volāns 'a flying chariot'

claustra rupta 'a broken lock'

perīculum metuendum 'a danger to be feared' (future passive participle)

The most memorable use of a future active participle is actually medieval, namely the inscription on the (supposed) grave of King Arthur:

Hīc iacet Artūrus, rēx quondam rēxque futūrus.[2]

'Here lies Arthur, king once and king to be.'

But Latin uses participles chiefly to construct participial clauses, e.g.:[3]

Alexander moriēns ānulum suum dederat Perdiccae. 'Alexander (when) dying had given his ring to Perdiccas.'

Dionȳsius tyrannus Syracūsīs expulsus Corinthī puerōs docēbat. 'The tyrant Dionysius (after being) driven out of Syracuse taught children at Corinth.'

Neither Mandarin nor Navajo has participles; they use relative clauses instead.

I noted in previous lessons that Navajo has no adjectives. Neither does Greenlandic; like Navajo, it has stative verbs, e.g. *mikivuq* '(s)he is small', *aputaippuq*

---

[1] I am grateful to Aaron Rubin for this example.

[2] This is actually a competent line of Classical Latin verse; apparently a monk at Glastonbury in the thirteenth century could acquire a decent education.

[3] These examples are from Gildersleeve and Lodge 1895: 426.

'it is snowless'. Unlike Navajo, Greenlandic also has no relative clauses, and by now you will have guessed that it uses participles instead, e.g.:

iglu mikissuq 'little house', lit. 'house being little'

In short, participles, relative clauses, and adjectives can all be used in the same ways. So far as I can tell, a language must have either participles or relative clauses, although it can do without adjectives.

There is a final detail of English grammar that illustrates one way that languages change over time. There are a number of adjectives like *molten* that look exactly like participles but can be used only as adjectives. That is, you can say

molten rock and *molten iron*,

but not

**The iron has molten.* nor **They have molten the iron.*

– you have to say

The iron has melted. and *They have melted the iron.*

In fact, you can't even say *molten ice; the only acceptable alternative is *melted ice*. The meaning of the adjective *molten* is narrow enough that it can only be applied to things that are ordinarily only solid in human experience. Then why does it look like a participle? The answer is that it once was a participle. The verb *melt* was an ablauting verb in Old English; when it was shifted into the default class, the old past participle *molten* survived in adjectival use. That is a fairly typical pattern of development: an old, largely superseded form survives in a secondary or derived function.

To Be Remembered from Lesson 25

Participles are adjectives, regularly formed from verbs, that retain some of the characteristics of verbs, such as the ability to govern objects. They are used

1) to construct complex verb phrases with auxiliaries;

2) as adjectives;

3) as the equivalent of relative clauses and clauses of other kinds.

Further Reading

Participial constructions are discussed in Quirk et al. 1980: 723–25, 740–42, 876–78
(English); Butt and Benjamin 2011: 304–7 (Spanish); Gildersleeve and Lodge 1895:
278–83, 285–86 (Latin); Gesenius and Kautzsch 1910: 355–62 (Hebrew).

26 | Comparative Constructions

Most English adjectives have COMPARATIVE and SUPERLATIVE forms. Except for a few irregular examples, comparatives of shorter and more basic adjectives end in *-er* and their superlatives in *-est*; longer adjectives typically use phrases with *more* and *most* (*more beautiful, most beautiful*). A comparative is typically followed by *than* and indicates a greater degree of whatever the adjective means; for instance, *bigger than a breadbox* takes the (typical) size of a breadbox as the standard of comparison and asserts enhanced bigness (i.e. greater size) relative to that standard. Superlatives are followed by standards of comparison expressed in a variety of ways and assert the greatest degree of whatever the adjective means within the entire universe of comparison, e.g. *biggest in the world, biggest of all.*

Surprisingly, such a comparison paradigm of adjectives is not very common among the world's languages. Many (though not all) languages belonging to the Indo-European family have such paradigms, but most other languages do not. They express comparison in a variety of ways.

Of our other sample languages, Latin resembles English most closely in this detail. Most adjectives have comparative and superlative forms; a few common adjectives have irregular comparison paradigms, as in English, although none of the actual words is historically connected to the corresponding English word. Thus we find:

altus, altior, altissimus	'high, higher, highest'
facilis, facilior, facillimus	'easy, easier, easiest'
bonus, melior, optimus	'good, better, best'

Latin has no phrasal comparison; all comparatives and superlatives are formed with suffixes. There is a particle *quam* which translates English 'than' more or less exactly, although the standard of comparison can often be put in the ablative case instead:

Mēnsa maior quam lectus est. | Mēnsa maior lectō est.
'The table is bigger than the bed.'

The standard of comparison with the superlative is also expressed in ways comparable to English.

Spanish is similar, but there are two significant differences. For most adjectives the comparative is formed simply by preposing the adverb *más* 'more'. Only a few of the irregular common comparatives of Latin survive; thus *mejor* is still the comparative of *bueno* 'good', and *mayor* is still the comparative of *grande* 'big' (although it has to compete with *más grande*), but 'higher' is *más alto*, 'easier' is *más fácil*, and so on. Secondly, the superlative form has been lost; to express the superlative, Spanish uses the comparative in a definite construction, typically with the definite article or a possessive adjective. For instance:

La mesa es más grande que la cama. | La mesa es mayor que la cama.
'The table is bigger than the bed.'

(The second alternative is mostly used in writing.)

Esta mesa es la más grande que yo he visto.
'This table is the biggest one that I've seen.'
Este es mi mejor amigo.
'This is my best friend.'

Otherwise the system is much like that of English and Latin.

Our other languages have similar constructions, but without any special forms of adjectives. Hebrew expresses 'than' by using *min-* 'from', e.g. (*Judges* 14.18):

Ma-   mmāṯōq middəḇaš?   'What is sweeter than honey?'
(what sweet   from-honey)

(*middəbaš* is assimilated from *min-dəbaš*). This actually resembles the Latin expression of the standard of comparison with the ablative case, since one of the core meanings of the ablative is 'from'. The superlative is expressed by using the definite article with the adjective (cf. Spanish), e.g. (*I Samuel* 16.11):

'Ōḏ šā'ar haqqāṭān. 'The youngest one still remains.'
(still is-left the-young)

The standard of comparison with superlatives can be expressed by the construct state construction, e.g. *gāḏōl hā'āreṣ* 'the greatest in the land'.

Mandarin expresses comparison with the preposition *bǐ* 'compared to, than', e.g. (Ho 2002: 114):

Fēijī bǐ huǒchē kuài. 飞机比火车快. '*The* plane is faster than the train.'
(airplane than train *fast*)

Superlatives are expressed by *zuì* 'most', e.g.:

Nǐ zuì měilì. 你最美丽. 'You are the most beautiful.'

It is clear that comparatives and superlatives are superfluous, and in fact even speakers of languages that have them don't always use them. I once overheard a conversation in which an Italian woman asserted that in Switzerland everything is regulated

dalle gran' genti alle piccole, piccole, piccole, piccole fin' alla formica,

literally 'from the big [i.e. important] people to the little, little, little, little all the way down to an ant'. She meant 'increasingly little', and she could have said *più piccole* (exactly like Spanish *más pequeñas*), yet she didn't (and didn't need to).

Navajo expression of comparison is different – as it must be, given that there are no adjectives, only stative verbs. Stative verbs have a special form, with an initial prefix *'á-* and a conjugation marker *-ł-*, which indicates that the state obtains to a greater-than-usual degree, e.g. (examples from Young and Morgan 1980, grammar p. 295):

Shimá nineez. 'My mother is tall.'
Shimá 'áníłnééz. 'My mother is very tall.'

Such verbs are used with the postposition -*lááh* 'beyond' to express comparison, e.g.:

   Díí 'éétsoh shilááh 'áníłnééz.   'This coat is taller than me.' (i.e. 'too big for me')

Superlatives are expressed in similar ways, e.g.:

   Shínaaí 'éí 'agháadi 'áníłnééz.   'My older brother is the tallest.' (-*ghá* 'furthest')

But there are also very different constructions that can express superlatives, e.g.:

   Shíjígó dinishwo'.   'I'm the fastest.'
   (literally: 'being (-*go*) on my (*shi-*) side, I am fast')

To Be Remembered from Lesson 26

Like possession, comparison can be expressed in a wide variety of ways; the system of each language must be learned separately.

27 | The Segmental Sounds of Human Languages

I hope that the preceding lessons have made the ways languages say things less mystifying, by demonstrating that they're all variations on common themes, so that the structure of any one language can help you understand the structure of others. But to a monolingual speaker, the worst is yet to come: the *sounds* of foreign languages seem to vary without limit, and it seems impossible to figure out how to pronounce some of them.

But, as usual, appearances are deceptive. It is actually easier to give a scientific description of speech sounds than of anything else about human language. In this lesson I will demonstrate how to do that, without going into every detail of every individual language. I will concentrate on the segmental sounds of languages – the consonants and vocalics; intonation and related matters will be discussed in the following lesson. Once you have read this (or maybe even before), you should look for a comparable description of the sounds of the language you are learning.

To begin with, we need to distinguish between physical description of the sounds, which is called PHONETICS, and the way a particular language organizes them, which is called PHONOLOGY. I will treat them in that order.

The easiest way to describe speech sounds as physical objects is to describe the ways in which they are made in the vocal apparatus: the larynx ("voice box" or "Adam's apple"), pharynx (immediately above the larynx), mouth, and nasal cavity. That approach, which I will use here, is called articulatory phonetics.

To make a speech sound you have to (1) set a column of air in motion in the vocal apparatus, (2) make it vibrate, and (3) manipulate its shape by moving parts of the vocal apparatus around. The usual way of setting the air in motion is controlled outward breathing; a substantial majority of languages (probably including the language you're studying) use only that airstream mechanism, and the remainder use it for most of their sounds. However, there are a few other ways of moving the air. Two of our languages, Navajo and (probably) Biblical Hebrew, also use an "ejective" mechanism, which can be explained as follows. You can close off the air completely in the larynx; in American English we do that in the middle of the colloquial interjection spelled "uh-uh" (meaning 'no'). That closure is called a glottal stop. To produce an ejective, you make a glottal stop and simultaneously close off the mouth at another place (see below), creating a sealed chamber of air in your mouth; then you jerk the larynx upward, compressing the air and forcing the mouth closure open, and you immediately release the glottal stop. The result is an ejective like Navajo *t'*, *tl'*, *ts'*, *ch'*, or *k'*; it appears that Biblical Hebrew *ṭ*, *ṣ*, and *q* were very similar to the first, third, and fifth of those Navajo consonants respectively.

Having set the column of air in motion, you need to make it vibrate. You do that with a pair of membrane flaps inside the larynx misleadingly called "vocal chords." There is one on the left and one on the right, and you tense them or relax them with the muscles that surround the larynx. If you let them hang loose, you get a voiceless sound, which is similar to a whispered sound; if you let them vibrate loosely together, you get a voiced sound. (There are several other things you can do with them, but most languages, including all our sample languages, use only voiced and voiceless sounds.) English sounds can be sorted into voiceless and voiced sets as follows:

voiceless: p t k ʧ   f θ s ʃ h   ʍ
voiced: b d ɡ ʤ   v ð z ʒ   m n ŋ l ɹ j w *and all vowels*

If you don't recognize some of the symbols in this list, that is because they are phonetic symbols of the International Phonetic Alphabet (IPA), designed to transcribe the sounds of any language unambiguously. That is especially necessary in dealing with English, whose spelling is grossly irregular (see Lesson 29). Here is an explanation of the unfamiliar symbols:

ʧ is the consonant at the beginning and end of *church*

θ is the consonant at the beginning of *thin*

ʃ is the consonant at the beginning of *ship*

ʍ is the consonant at the beginning of *which* (but most speakers of English actually replace it with [w], as in *witch* – I certainly do)

ɡ is the consonant at the beginning of *give* (sometimes called "hard g")

dʒ is the consonant at the beginning and end of *judge* ("soft g", as in *gin*)

ð is the consonant at the beginning of *then*

ʒ is the consonant in the middle of *measure, leisure, vision,* etc.

ŋ is the "ng" of *sing* and *singer* (not *finger* – that word has [ŋg] – listen to it!)

ɹ is the peculiar English *r* at the beginning of words

j is the consonant at the beginning of *yes* (the IPA uses [y] for something totally different)

To a first approximation, voiceless sounds are whispered, while voiced sounds are buzzed. You can hear the difference by putting your fingers firmly in your ears and saying, over and over, "ssszzzssszzzssszzz..." When you pronounce the s's, you'll hear almost nothing, but when you pronounce the z's, you'll hear a buzz or a roar. That's because you're forcing yourself to hear your own speech through the bones of your head (since you've closed off the airways), and voiced sounds propagate through dense media (such as water or bone) much better than voiceless sounds do. If you'd feel embarrassed to be discovered hissing and buzzing with your fingers in your ears, try putting the tips of a couple of fingers on your Adam's apple and producing the same sequence of sounds; you should feel much more vibration on the voiced z's than on the voiceless s's.

Note that all vowels are voiced in English, and in an overwhelming majority of other languages (though not in all).

Once the airstream gets past the vocal chords and is set in vibration (either voiced or voiceless), it enters the pharynx, the common passage that will divide into the mouth and the nasal passage a little further up. Almost the only way you can make a speech sound in the pharynx is by pulling the tongue back so as to narrow the pharynx and create turbulence in the airstream. Of our languages, only Hebrew avails itself of that option; the voiceless pharyngeal consonant is the one transliterated as *ḥ*, while the voiced pharyngeal is '. Both are difficult to pronounce if your native language doesn't have such consonants, but from the description just given, you can teach yourself to make a pretty good approximation.

Above the pharynx the vocal apparatus divides into the mouth and the nasal passage. You have no control over what happens inside the nasal passage, but you can close it off or leave it open. If you open your mouth very wide in front of a mirror, you'll see that at the back the roof of the mouth hangs free. That part is the velum, or "soft palate." You can pull it up and back to close off the nasal passage (although it's quite difficult to feel that that's what you're doing). If you do that, you make non-nasal (or oral) sounds, and most speech sounds are non-nasal; if you let the velum hang free, so that the nasal passage remains open, you make nasal sounds. The English consonants [m n ŋ] are nasal, and so are the corresponding consonants in our other languages; the French nasal vowels spelled *in, un, an, on* are also made with the velum down and the nasal passage open.

If all three of those English consonants are nasal, what distinguishes them? To make a nasal consonant, you not only leave the nasal passage open: you also make a complete closure in the mouth, so that the airstream passes only through the nose. The place where you make the closure is called the place of articulation, and our three nasal consonants are made at three different places of articulation. [m] is a bilabial consonant, made by closing the lips tightly, as you can see by looking in a mirror; [ŋ] is a velar consonant, made by raising the back of the tongue until it contacts the front part of the velum, closing off the mouth at that point. (That's much harder to see, but you might be able to feel yourself making that closure.) Depending on the language, [n] is either a dental nasal, made by pressing the tip of the tongue against the backs of the upper front teeth to make a closure at that point, or an alveolar nasal, with the closure made against the lower side of the ridge that runs across the mouth right behind the upper front teeth. (English has an alveolar nasal; French has a dental nasal. In some languages, such as Spanish, both pronunciations are used, depending on what sounds are adjacent in the word. The situation in ancient languages is often unclear.) In an overwhelming majority of languages, including all of ours, all nasal consonants are voiced.

But there are more than three places of articulation in the mouth; in fact there are well over a dozen. For instance, Spanish *ñ* is a palatal nasal, with the closure made by raising the front part of the body of the tongue against the (hard) palate, the bony plate that runs back from the ridge behind the upper front teeth. (You can feel it by pressing against the roof of your mouth with your thumb, and you can feel where it ends and the velum begins.) Places of articulation will be discussed further below.

There is a much greater variety of non-nasal consonants because you can do a variety of things at different places of articulation; the most important alternatives are the following. If you stop the airstream completely there is a split-second of total silence (or near-silence, if the consonant is voiced), because the nasal passage is closed off too and the air has nowhere to go. When you release the closure, the result is a stop consonant. English has a pair of stops, voiceless and voiced, at each of the places of articulation where it also has a nasal: bilabial [p b m], alveolar [t d n], and velar [k g ŋ]. That is not universal, but it is typical.

As you might expect, it requires extra effort to make the voicing gesture in the throat when the mouth is completely closed off. In spite of that, Spanish *b, d, g* are completely voiced, and it is believed that the corresponding Latin and Biblical Hebrew consonants were fully voiced as well. But English *b, d, g* are very weakly voiced, especially at the beginning of a word. The contrast with *p, t, k* in word-initial position is maintained by aspirating *p, t,* and *k*; that is, not only are those consonants fully voiceless, but their voicelessness laps over into the following vowel or consonant, so that it sounds like there is a brief *h* after the *p, t,* or *k*. Mandarin and Navajo take that one step further: Mandarin *p, t, k, c, ch, q* are always aspirated, while *b, d, g* are completely voiceless (but not aspirated); Navajo *t, k, ts, ch, tł* are heavily aspirated (especially *t* and *k*), while *b, d, g* are completely voiceless, as in Mandarin.

Instead of closing the airstream off completely, it is possible to narrow it so much that the air is forced through a tiny opening, creating turbulence. Consonants produced in that manner are called fricatives. Fricatives can be produced at almost any place of articulation, whereas at some it is difficult to produce stops. For instance, if you bring the lower lip into contact with the upper teeth, making a labiodental closure, you will find it difficult to close off the airstream completely, because the air leaks out at the bottom of the teeth; but making labiodental fricatives is easy, and English has a pair, voiceless [f] and voiced [v]. Other voiceless–voiced pairs of English fricatives are dental [θ ð], alveolar [s z], and postalveolar [ʃ ʒ] (made by arching the front part of the body of the tongue and pushing it into the hollow behind the upper tooth ridge). In addition, there is a voiceless glottal fricative [h], made simply by the voiceless gesture in the larynx (see above). The range of fricatives our six languages exhibit is very wide, and the possible range is even wider. Here is a comparative chart, with fricatives in the languages other than English given in standard spelling or transcription. Where two consonants are listed in a single cell, the first is voiceless and the second voiced, separated by a comma; when only one or the other occurs in a language, it is placed to the left or right of a comma.

	E	S	L	H	N	M
bilabial		, b		p̄, ƀ		
labiodental	f, v	f,	f,			f,
dental	θ, ð	z, d		ṭ, đ		
alveolar	s, z	s,	s,	s, z	s, z	s,
lateral alveolar				ś,	ł, l	
alveolo-palatal						x,
postalveolar	ʃ, ʒ			š,	sh, zh	sh,
velar		j, g		ḳ, g	h, gh	h,
pharyngeal				ḥ, ʻ		
glottal	h,		h,	h,	h,	

Some notes on this table are necessary, as follows.

Spanish *b, d, g* are fricatives only when preceded by vowels or (in the case of *b* and *g*) by *r* or *l*; otherwise they are fully voiced stops (see above). Spanish *z* (spelled *c* before *e* or *i*) is dental [θ] only in Spain; in the Americas it is identical with *s*.

Navajo *h* is pronounced as velar [x] (like the last consonant of the German name *Bach*) at the beginning of stem syllables, but otherwise as [h], so far as I can tell from the literature. Laterals are made by closing off the mouth down the middle and letting the air flow along one or both sides, next to the teeth; they are fricatives if the air passage is narrow enough. Voiceless *l* is clearly a fricative; voiced *l* is sometimes said to be an approximant, but it has more friction than the *l* 's of our other languages (on which see below).

Mandarin *x* differs from *sh* mainly by tongue shape: whereas *sh* is much like the corresponding English sound, for *x* the tip of the tongue is tucked in behind the lower teeth and the front of the body of the tongue is raised toward the front of the roof of the mouth.

It is possible to run a stop and a fricative (in that order) together to make an affricate; English examples are [ʧ dʒ]. Affricates often (though not always) appear instead of stops in places of articulation where it is difficult to make a stop. The English affricates are cases in point; so is German [pf]. Of our sample languages, Navajo has affricates *ts, tł, ch* (aspirated), *dz, dl, j* (partly voiced) and *ts', tł', ch'* (glottalized) at the same positions as the corresponding fricatives; Mandarin has *c, q, ch* (aspirated) and *z, j, zh* (partly voiced) at the same positions as the corresponding fricatives; Biblical Hebrew apparently had *ṣ* (glottalized) at the same position as *s* and *z*.

Languages use a wide array of consonants in which the closure is not even great enough to produce a fricative; they are collectively called approximants, and they are usually (though not always) voiced. Lateral approximants are made by a closure down the midline of the mouth, lowering one or both sides of the tongue so that the air can pass unimpeded along the side teeth; all l-sounds are laterals. Some r-sounds, such as the English *r* [ɹ], are approximants. Others are trills, flaps, or taps made at various places of articulation; there is a great deal of variation between languages' r-sounds, and many are difficult for foreigners to learn to produce. English [ɹ] is difficult even for native learners; it is often the last consonant acquired.

Vocalics are made with the mouth even more open than for approximants. The only place where you can open your mouth wide enough to make a vocalic is in the middle, the region where palatal and velar consonants are made. If a vocalic can be pronounced as a separate syllable it is called a vowel, and most vocalics are vowels. They are classified along a number of parameters, as follows:

1) *height*, i.e. how high the highest part of the tongue is bunched up. If it is raised as high as possible for a vowel, that is a high vowel; Spanish [i] and [u] are high vowels. If it is as low as possible, that is a low vowel; Spanish [a] is a low vowel. There are several distinguishable heights in between.
2) *frontness*, i.e. whether the highest part of the tongue is in the front, under the hard palate, or in the back, under the velum, or somewhere in between.

Spanish [i] and [e] are front vowels; [u] and [o] are back vowels; low [a] is a central vowel.

3) *roundness*, i.e. whether the lips are rounded. Spanish [u] and [o] are round as well as back, whereas the other Spanish vowels are unround. That is typical but not universal; for instance, German *ü* [y] and *ö* [ø] are front round vowels, while the English vowel of *cup* (IPA symbol [ʌ]) is a back unround vowel.

4) *length*. Some languages, including Navajo, German, Latin, and (at an early stage) Biblical Hebrew, distinguish between long and short vowels. The crucial distinction is that the long vowels actually take longer to say – usually at least one-and-a-half times as long as the short vowels. Sometimes there is no other difference. For instance, the difference between German *Masse* [mɑsə] 'mass, lump' and *Maße* [mɑ:sə] 'measures' is that the stressed vowel of the second word is much longer than that of the first; to an English ear, the first sounds a bit clipped, while the second sounds drawled.

5) *nasalization*. Some languages, such as French, Portuguese, and Hindi, have vowels pronounced with the nasal passage open (see above).

There are various other, less common parameters that a language can use to distinguish its vowels.

Nonsyllabic vocalics are often called semivowels; English has two or three, namely [j], which is a nonsyllabic version of high front unround [i]; [w], which is a nonsyllabic version of high back round [u]; and, for some speakers, [ʍ], which is a voiceless *w*.

It seems superfluous to go into further detail about phonetics here. Whatever language you are learning, you should look for a scientific description of its speech sounds along the lines sketched above; it will help you learn to pronounce them. Wikipedia provides thumbnail phonetic descriptions for a large number of languages.

Phonetics is very important, but it is not the whole story. In the (incomplete) description of the sounds of English and our other languages sketched above, I deliberately omitted a major complication: the pronunciation of any given speech sound varies a great deal, even in the speech of a single native speaker. How, then, do speakers manage to keep the sounds of their language straight?

The basic principle is that, in each language, some differences between sounds are crucial, while the rest are irrelevant. Crucial differences are called phonemic distinctions, and they are the differences used to distinguish between different words and utterances. Very importantly, each language makes its own phonemic distinctions; the basic phonetic framework is universal, but phonemic distinctions are not. Here is an example. In English the difference between the alveolar nasal [n] and the velar nasal [ŋ] is phonemic and is used to distinguish words; for instance, *kin*, with an alveolar [n], is a different word from *king*, with a velar [ŋ]. We express that situation by saying the /n/ and /ŋ/ are two different PHONEMES in English, and we write them between slashes. Spanish has the same two nasals, but they are not different phonemes. Velar [ŋ] occurs when a velar consonant follows immediately, e.g. in *cinco* [siŋko][1] 'five', *tengo* [teŋgo] 'I have', and *lonja* [loŋxa][2] 'exchange'. In addition, some speakers use [ŋ] in word-final position, while others use [n]; thus *pan* 'bread' can be heard both as [pan] and as [paŋ]. Elsewhere [n] occurs.[3] The difference between [n] and [ŋ] is never used to distinguish one word from another. We say that there is a single phoneme /n/, and that velar [ŋ] is merely an allophone (conditioned pronunciation) of /n/ that occurs in certain positions in the word.

Most brief descriptions of the sounds of a foreign language for learners actually list the phonemes of the language, giving phonetic information about the default, or usual, pronunciations of the phonemes. (That is what I have done in this lesson, for the most part.) Such a strategy makes sense because the phonemic structure of a language's sound system is the most important thing about it. If you confuse two or more of a language's phonemes, you might not be understood. If you distinguish them all, but your reproductions of the phonetic details are a little off for some of them, you will probably be understood, although native speakers will know that you're a foreigner and say that you speak "with an accent."

---

[1] American Spanish; in Castilian Spanish, [θiŋko].

[2] [x] is a voiceless velar fricative in the pronunciation of Spanish described here; for many speakers it is pronounced further back in the mouth, and in that case so is the nasal immediately preceding it.

[3] This statement is oversimplified; in fact /n/ is dental when a dental stop follows immediately, labiodental when /f/ follows immediately, and so on. Those details are not relevant to the point at hand.

To Be Remembered from Lesson 27

The single most important thing to be remembered from this lesson is the distinction between phonetics – the physical description of speech sounds – and phonology, especially the principle of phonemic contrast.

Further Reading

Good, comprehensive introductions to phonetics are Johnson 2003 and Ladefoged 2015. A comprehensive and detailed summary of the phonetics of the world's languages is provided by Ladefoged and Maddieson 1996.

28 | Prosody

The preceding lesson discussed the consonants and vocalics of human languages, which we perceive as a sequence of discrete sounds. But there are other aspects of a language's sounds which do not seem to be part of that sequence; instead they are spread across the sequence, or even seem to float on top of it. Those phenomena are collectively called prosody; they include stress, pitch, timing, and other, more obscure phenomena that we do not need to discuss here.

English clearly has a system of stress: some syllables, called stressed syllables, are spoken more loudly than others. It is mostly the loudness of stressed syllables that native speakers of English perceive. But in fact English stressed syllables are usually also longer than unstressed syllables – that is, they actually take longer to say – and they are also often spoken on a higher pitch than the syllables around them.

There are several different degrees of stress in English. For instance, in long words such as

ínterdìgitătion

there can be as many as three degrees of stress: the main stress is on the second-to-last syllable, marked with ˝; there is a secondary stress on the first syllable, marked with an acute accent; and there is a tertiary stress on the third syllable, marked with a grave accent. The remaining syllables are completely unstressed. In addition, each clause has a larger stress pattern into which the stress patterns of the individual words fit. In some cases the stress of a word shifts so that it fits better into the phrasal or sentential pattern (e.g. *Tènnessée*, but *Ténnessèe whìskey*).

All these aspects of stress are rule-governed, and the rules are complex. However, stress in English is not completely predictable, because it is possible to change the meaning or function of a word by shifting its stress from one syllable to another. For instance, *pervért*, with the stress on the second syllable, is a verb, whereas *pérvert*, with the stress on the first syllable, is a noun meaning 'perverted person' or 'deviant person'. So in English you start with words that have stresses of their own and build the prosody of phrases and clauses from them by rule.

An English utterance also has a pitch contour, called an "intonation" pattern. English intonation is much more variable than English stress. For instance, the pitch commonly rises toward the end of a question, while it falls toward the end of a clause of another type; but some people routinely produce sequences of statements each with a rising intonation, as if asking for the hearer's acceptance of what they're saying, and in exceptional circumstances it is possible to produce a question with a falling intonation.

Spanish likewise has a stress system, but it appears to be simpler than that of English. Only one syllable of a major word is stressed, and it is always one of the last three syllables. As in English, stress is contrastive; cf. e.g. present subjunctive *cante* '(that) (s)he sing', with stress on the first syllable, vs. preterite indicative *canté* 'I sang', with stress on the last syllable. (There is a well-developed system for marking stress in written Spanish, organized so as to use as few accent marks as possible.)

In spite of the fact that they both have stress systems, spoken English and spoken Spanish do not sound much alike. That is partly because English unstressed vowels are greatly reduced – often all the way to the indistinct vowel [ə] – whereas in Spanish they are not. But it is also the case that in English the amount of time between each pair of *stressed* syllables in an utterance tends to be roughly equal, so that if there are many unstressed syllables in between, we hurry over them, whereas if there is only one, we tend to drag it out. Phonologists describe that phenomenon by saying that English is "stress-timed." Spanish certainly is not stress-timed; the time allotted to each syllable, stressed or unstressed, is less unequal than in English. Not that the syllables are exactly equal: scientific measurement of natural speech shows clearly that stressed syllables are longer than unstressed syllables in Spanish, roughly as in English. But the unstressed syllables are not hurried or mumbled in Spanish, and it makes some sense to suggest that Spanish is "syllable-timed."

We know a good deal about the stress systems of Biblical Hebrew and Classical Latin because of the Masoretic tradition and the works of the ancient Roman grammarians respectively. A full text of the Hebrew Bible includes an elaborate system of accent marks that tell the reader not only the prosody of each word and verse, but even the structure of the verses. We can say with confidence that the Biblical Hebrew system of stress was roughly like that of English in general, though of course different in detail. Basic word stress was contrastive, although pairs of words distinguished only by stress are rare; an example is *qā́mā* 'she arose' vs. *qāmā́* 'arising (fem.)'.[1] As in English, the stress patterns of individual words were fitted into the larger stress pattern of the utterance, and there were some systematic shifts. For a good exploration of the way in which the traditional system of accents reveals the prosodic structure of Biblical Hebrew, see Dresher 1994.

Latin stress, by contrast, was almost entirely automatic, dictated by syllable structure. A syllable containing a long vowel or a diphthong, or a short vowel followed by two consonants (with certain principled exceptions), is said to be heavy; a syllable containing a short vowel followed by only one consonant (or no consonant) is said to be light. Stress is assigned as follows:

monosyllabic major words are always stressed;

disyllabic words are always stressed on the initial syllable;

if a word has three or more syllables, it is stressed on the second-to-last syllable if that syllable is heavy, otherwise on the third-to-last syllable (regardless of weight).

Exceptions to those rules are very few and are easily specified and learned.

[1] I am grateful to Aaron Rubin for this example.

In our remaining languages prosody is dominated by pitch rather than stress. Both are tone languages, in which every syllable (in principle) has an inherent pitch, called a tone.

Navajo has no stress pattern: all syllables are equally stressed. In fact, all syllables are treated as heavy, according to the informal definition just given for Latin; if a syllable is underlyingly light, the consonant following its short vowel is automatically doubled in pronunciation so as to make it heavy. For instance, the verb form

shee'ék'idahalta'dooleeł 'they will be keeping company with me'

(Sapir and Hoijer 1942: 16)

is pronounced

shee-'ék-k'id-dah-hal-ta'-doo-leeł,

with the second, third, and fourth syllables made heavy by doubling the consonant after the short vowel. Every vowel has a tone; so does the syllable *n*, which is a reduced form of *ni*. In the case of a short vowel the tone can only be high or low; high tone is written with an acute accent, while low tone is unmarked. For a long vowel or diphthong there are four contrastive tones: *áá* (high), *aa* (low), *áa* (falling), *aá* (rising), although the falling and rising tones are derived by vowel contraction and tone shift rules. Because of its unusual prosodic structure, spoken Navajo sounds very unlike a European language.

Mandarin has four tones, represented by marks over the vowels in the pinyin system of Romanization: *ā* (high level), *á* (fairly high rising, often somewhat drawled), *ǎ* (low with a dip in the middle), *à* (sharply falling, often somewhat clipped). Monosyllabic major words are all stressed; the second elements of compounds are sometimes destressed, and some (but not all) can lose their tones and become toneless. Particles are also often destressed and toneless. Thus stress plays some role in Mandarin prosody, but it is not as pervasive as tone. Spoken Mandarin also sounds very unlike a European language.

The tones of tone languages are not absolute pitches: they are high or low relative to adjacent syllables in the same utterance. The overall pitch of the voice tends to decrease over the length of an utterance, so that a high tone on the last syllable can actually be lower in pitch than a low tone early in the utterance.

There is at least one other way that a language can organize its prosody, namely by pitch accent. Whereas every syllable in a tone language has an inherent tone, in a pitch accent system only one syllable per word is singled out for special treatment. In other words, pitch accent is like stress accent, except that *only* pitch marks an accented syllable. The pitch accent language best known to me is Ancient Greek, whose system was fairly well described by native-speaker grammarians. Among modern languages, Japanese has a pitch accent system.

29 | Writing Systems

Living human languages are primarily spoken, and a language cannot be fully living unless it is spoken by native speakers who learned it in childhood. Writing is not language; writing is a *representation* of (some of) a language's utterances. That is probably not what they taught you in school. The benefits of being literate are so overwhelming (and the handicap of being functionally illiterate is so crippling) that schoolteachers are anxious to exalt writing as much as possible. In addition, people in many cultures are taught to write a formal version of their language that is not quite the same as what anyone speaks; often it is somewhat out of date and somewhat artificial. It is easy, but mistaken, to get the impression that that artificial written version is somehow "more real" than the spoken language we all use, whereas in fact the reverse is true. In short, writing is derivative, and that is why I deal with it only after discussing language sounds.

Most languages are written with alphabets. The principle of alphabetic writing is simple: each phoneme of a language (see Lesson 27) should be represented consistently by a distinct symbol, called a letter. Some languages, such as Greenlandic, have fully phonemic writing systems. Others come close; for instance, the only way in which Navajo orthography (i.e. spelling) and the pinyin system of transcribing Mandarin depart from the phonemic principle is that they must use two symbols together[1] for some phonemes, because there are not enough letters in the Roman alphabet to spell all their phonemes.

The orthographies of some other languages depart from the phonemic principle in various systematic ways. For instance, standard Classical Latin orthography does not mark vowel length (although it is marked in grammars and dictionaries, and in this book); in addition, the semivowels /j/ and /w/ are written with the symbols for the corresponding high vowels, *i* and *u* (although the latter is replaced by *v* in some modern publications, including this book), and /kw/ is written *qu*. The ancient Hebrew alphabet wrote only the consonants, like many other Semitic writing systems, although a system of marks indicating vowels and accents was eventually devised to supplement the letters. For historical reasons Spanish spells its velar stops as *qu* and *gu* before front vowels, but as *c* and *g* elsewhere, and there are other minor complications in the Spanish system.

Unsystematic departures from the phonemic principle also occur, and unfortunately English orthography is full of them; in fact it is difficult to find a language written in an alphabet whose orthography is more confused than that of English (although Modern Irish – i.e. Gaelic – is a plausible candidate). That is partly the result of historical accidents; for instance, the vowels of *see* and *sea, here* and *hear, meet* and *meat*, etc., merged (i.e. became identical) sometime in the sixteenth century, but the spelling of the words was never adjusted to take account of that fact – partly because of the sheer weight of tradition, but also partly because the vowel merger took a long time to go to completion, with different dialects in competition for standard status over several generations. But there are also details of English spelling that never made phonemic sense. For instance, *son* and *sun* have had the same vowel since the beginning of Old English (and even earlier), yet the vowels are now spelled differently; conversely, the contrast between the [θ] of *ether* and the [ð] of *either* has been in place since sometime early in the fifteenth century, yet the spelling has never been adjusted to reflect that, although it would be easy and unambiguous to spell [ð] with *dh* rather than *th*. It seems reasonable to ask why English has never undergone a spelling reform, as most European languages have. One reason is that there has never been an institution that could enforce such a reform in

---

[1] In Navajo, three for some ejective consonants, e.g. *tl'*, *ts'*, *ch'*.

English-speaking countries. Another is more practical, however: by this point a consistent reform would have to make so many changes that anyone trained in the new, phonemically correct system would find it difficult to read anything currently written in English. Since English has now become the world's international language, ubiquitous on the internet, that would be a disaster. We're stuck with just about the worst orthography in the world.

There are alternatives to alphabets. In the ancient world they were common, but in the modern world they have become rare, simply because a properly phonemic alphabet is so easy to learn and use. One major holdout is the system of Chinese characters. A Chinese character writes a syllable that has a specified pronunciation and meaning, i.e. a word (or part of a compound word, or a particle). Thus in principle there has to be a separate character for each word, and the number of characters to be learned is very large. There seems to be a consensus that to read a newspaper you have to be able to recognize about 3,000 characters; for anything more complex or specialized the required number is much larger.

Foreigners inevitably wonder why Chinese society continues to use so complex a system of writing. Tradition is only part of the answer. For one thing, the large number of characters to be learned is not so much of a problem if you learned hundreds of them in school as a child, and of course that is how most native speakers of Chinese languages learned them. In addition, the system is structured, although its structure is complex and quirky (like so much else in human culture); an educated native speaker of Mandarin once advised me that when you've learned about 500 characters the system begins to make sense, and you can begin to make more rapid progress. There are also two major advantages to the system of characters that are not likely to be apparent to a foreigner. There are between seven and ten Chinese languages, all obviously related, but different enough from one another that their speakers cannot understand each other. (In fact, within some of the more obscure Chinese languages, dialect differences can also be dramatic: a native speaker of Gàn from Jiāngxī province once told me that people from villages only 50 miles apart within the province have great difficulty understanding each other.) But all those languages share a large proportion of their core vocabulary, so that a system that writes words rather than sounds makes written Chinese largely intelligible across the languages. In addition, many Chinese languages, including Mandarin, have undergone so many mergers of sounds (like the English *meet–meat* merger mentioned above) that they are full of homonyms that can cause ambiguity; a system that writes sounds and meanings together is less ambiguous. For instance, there are three common verbs pronounced *zuò*; the writing system distinguishes them:

> *zuò* 作 'do, make, compose'   *zuò* 做 'work, make'[2]   *zuò* 坐 'sit'

There are more than a dozen common words pronounced *jī*, meaning things as various as 'muscles', 'hungry', 'odd (number)', 'footprints', etc., and each is written with its own character. It is not all that surprising that native speakers of Chinese languages generally prefer their writing system to an alphabet.

It is also possible to write with a syllabary, in which each syllable is represented by a different symbol without regard to meaning. James Evans, working with the Cree of northern Canada, who speak an Algonkian language, invented a syllabary to write their language; it has been so successful that various of their neighbors have borrowed and adapted it, including peoples speaking unrelated languages such as Inuktitut (an Eskimoan language) and Carrier (an Athabaskan language). Sequoyah invented a syllabary to write his native Cherokee (an Iroquoian language) that is likewise still in use.

Finally, it is possible to write with a mixed system. The Japanese also invented a syllabary that is perfectly adapted to write their language, and it would be possible to write Japanese just with the syllabary; but they continue to use it in conjunction with Chinese characters that had previously been adapted to write Japanese (with only partial success, as the structures of the languages are very different). Mixed writing systems are generally the most difficult to learn and use; so far as I know, the Japanese system is the only one still in widespread use.

Since writing is merely a representation of language, it is possible to write a language in more than one writing system. Mandarin can be written not only in characters, but also in Roman letters; the pinyin system used throughout this book is now the standard Roman orthography for Mandarin. It would be equally

---

[2] There is some overlap in meaning between this verb and the preceding one, but they are different words, and there are circumstances in which only one of the two is acceptable. They also make largely different sets of compound words.

possible to write English with characters, or with a mixed system like that of Japanese. Whether that would be any harder to use than our inconsistent alphabetic orthography is a good question, but, for all the obvious reasons, it's not going to happen – any more than the Chinese will ever give up writing with characters.

To Be Remembered from Lesson 29

Writing is a representation of language; it is always derivative of speech (sometimes the speech of the past). Because that is true, it is possible to write any language in any system of writing that can represent the language's phonemes, syllables, or words adequately.

30 | The Lexicon

Although the rules of grammar are the most distinctive part of any human language, a language must also have words for the rules of grammar to manipulate; otherwise there is no material to build sentences from. Linguists call a language's fund of words its lexicon. Lexical items ("words") are like tokens to which meanings are arbitrarily assigned; you can reassign their meanings, or even replace them entirely, with minimal impact on the language's grammar. For the most part, their pronunciations are even more arbitrary than their meanings; for instance, there is no inherent reason the most useful animal in preindustrial societies should be called *horse, caballo, equus, sūs, łį́į́, mǎ*, or anything else.

Nevertheless lexical items do have at least a bit of structure. They have phonological structures, which (as the last two lessons have shown) are distinctive for each language. Some also have internal structure because they are composed of smaller units, called MORPHEMES. (A lexical item that cannot be decomposed into smaller meaningful units is composed of only one morpheme; morphemes are to words as clauses are to sentences.) In general, complex words are of two types. Some are compounds, composed of two or more major words; English examples include *blackbird, tenderfoot, two-faced, withstand* (in which *with* means 'against', as in *fight with*), *shovel-ready*, and so forth. Others are derived from other words with affixes that are not themselves freestanding words; English examples include *pre-wash, kindness, kingdom, etherize*, etc. Of course, a lexical item can exhibit both types of structure, like English *gentlemanliness*, and there are various groups of words in various languages that are difficult to analyze, but on the whole the rough dichotomy between compounding and derivation gives a fair idea of what the structure of complex words is like.

Languages do not use compounding and derivation equally. Mandarin has thousands of compounds but few derived words. Biblical Hebrew has a fair number of derived words but few, if any, compounds. Latin has both, but most of the compounds are preposition-plus-verb, comparable to English *withstand*; otherwise compounds are rare, and they have remained fairly rare in Spanish. But regardless of their structure, commonly used complex words tend to acquire idiosyncratic meanings of their own, not derivable from the meanings of their parts. English *gentleman* is a case in point: its first member *gentle* no longer means 'member of the gentry', as it did when the compound was formed, and even if we make allowance for that and use *gentle* in its original meaning, *gentleman* no longer means 'male member of the gentry'. Even *kindness* is unusual in that it can mean a single kind act (e.g. *their many kindnesses to me*), whereas most nouns in *-ness* indicate only abstractions. For discussion of that phenomenon in depth, see Jackendoff 1975.

Because lexical items are, in effect, tokens dropped into "slots" provided by the syntax, languages can and do borrow words from one another. English is notorious for the ease with which it borrows foreign words, but in fact all modern European languages have borrowed numerous words from other languages (including each other). They have even borrowed words from Latin and Ancient Greek, two languages that have had no native speakers for many centuries.[1] In Spanish and the other Romance languages, one can find, side by side, lexical items that were passed down by native acquisition over the centuries, slowly undergoing changes of various kinds, and "the same" words re-borrowed from

---

[1] Modern Greek is of course directly descended from Ancient Greek, but the two languages are about as different from one another as Italian is from Latin, and for the same reason: so long as a language remains alive, it will change from generation to generation. Language change is universal and unstoppable.

Latin in the Middle Ages and the Renaissance. For instance, Latin *clāmāre* 'to shout' developed into Spanish *llamar* 'to call' over the centuries, but the same verb was re-borrowed as *clamar* 'to shout' relatively recently. Latin also borrowed a considerable number of words from the languages with which it was in contact, most obviously Greek, but also Etruscan, Gaulish, and other ancient languages. In many cases we can tell that a Latin word is not native because of its unusual shape, or because of its distribution among the languages of the ancient Mediterranean, but we can't identify the source of the borrowing because our attestation of ancient languages is too sparse; well-known examples include *mālum* 'apple', *porrum* 'leek', *rosa* 'rose', and *ebur* 'ivory'.

Not all languages borrow words freely. In general, if it is difficult to fit a borrowed word into the morphosyntax or phonology of the language, borrowing will be avoided; instead, a new word will be coined from native resources (see above). For that reason languages which have elaborate systems of verb inflection borrow few verbs, and/or have a systematic default way of inflecting borrowed verbs; for instance, borrowed verbs in German normally have infinitives in *-ieren* and are placed in the default inflectional class, while borrowed verbs in Russian normally have infinitives ending in *-irovat'*. Navajo has borrowed few, if any, verbs; Mandarin has borrowed few words of any kind in recent centuries because it is difficult to fit them into the tightly constrained phonological system.

Languages' lexica differ noticeably in size. The English lexicon is enormous, and those of German and Ancient Greek are also very large. The Classical Latin lexicon, by contrast, is smaller than that of many languages – definitely smaller than the lexica of its descendants – and the Biblical Hebrew lexicon is smaller still. Strikingly, the size of a language's lexicon makes no practical difference; all human languages have ways of saying everything their native speakers need to say, even if some are a bit less concise because more words must occasionally be used. Of course to some extent that's because lexica are less different in practice than in theory. Much of the huge English lexicon amounts to sets of specialized words used only in certain professions or sciences, and a significant portion is more or less obsolete words occurring only in poetry or in elevated speech; a typical speaker of English, even if educated, uses only a few thousand words most of the time. But it still seems to be true that a typical speaker of Classical Latin, for instance, got by with a smaller vocabulary than a typical speaker of Ancient Greek, and it's definitely true that many English compound words must be expressed by short phrases in French or Spanish, while some German compounds must be expressed by phrases even in English.

The size of a language's lexicon also has no effect on the quality of its verbal art: great poetry has been composed in every one of our six sample languages[2] and in hundreds of others. However, that should be no surprise. Verbal art is about manipulating the structures of a language for effect, no matter what those structures might be, and every language gives a competent poet more than enough to work with.

---

[2] Traditional Navajo poetry, like Biblical Hebrew poetry, is religious.

Epilogue: "Bad Grammar"

Everyone has at least one native dialect, learned in early childhood by the normal process of native language acquisition; many people have two or more native dialects. For some people their native dialect, or at least one of their native dialects, is a standard dialect of an official language. Other people's native dialects have no official status and are called "nonstandard." But every dialect of every language, standard or not, has a rigidly fixed grammar with precise rules. The widespread notion that nonstandard dialects are not fully rule-governed is just plain wrong, as any competent linguist can demonstrate. For instance, as we saw in Lesson 20, the multiple negatives of nonstandard English dialects are not capricious or "illogical": they simply obey a set of rules different from those of standard English – and it shouldn't surprise you that the rules governing the use of negatives in nonstandard English are the same as those of standard Spanish and Italian and Ancient Greek (while the more unconstrained system of Old and Middle English is like that of Russian).

Native speakers of a dialect have a perfect, but unconscious, knowledge of its rules; they do not consistently make grammatical mistakes when speaking it. Of course people make slips of the tongue, and we all occasionally start complex sentences and then reconsider in the middle, but people correct those occasional errors, usually immediately. It is literally *not possible* for a person to speak his or her native dialect badly. So where does the schoolroom notion of "bad grammar" come from?

The dialects we are taught to speak and write in schools are usually standard dialects of whatever language is dominant in a given society. Students who were not lucky enough to learn the relevant standard dialect natively in early childhood have to acquire it in school – just when their ability to acquire a new dialect natively is beginning to decline (although native acquisition won't become totally impossible for a few more years). Teachers are understandably anxious to motivate them to learn it, because it makes a big difference – in most societies your job opportunities will be limited if you can't use the standard dialect fluently – and they don't have unlimited time. It's not surprising that some resort to telling the native speakers of nonstandard dialects that their English (for example) is "bad," and that they must learn "good English." Whether that's an effective way to motivate the students is a separate question, and I suspect that good teachers would say it isn't. (I don't recall such stigmatization from my own schooling, but I was in school in the 1960s, when all sorts of traditional practices were being questioned.) But the most important point is that all such value judgments about language are *social* (or perhaps political) judgments. They have nothing to do with the structure of a dialect, or with logic, or with how expressive a dialect is, and so on. From those standpoints, all dialects of all languages are equal, whether they have official status anywhere or not.

So far, so good: it's easy to criticize teachers for stigmatizing nonstandard dialects, but at least their objectives make sense. Much less defensible are the fulminations of newspaper columnists and popular authors about "bad English."[1] The pretense that they're trying to educate the public seems pretty thin to me; I think it more likely that they're expressing the hostility (or maybe the anxiety) of an educated class toward everyone else. You can easily infer what a liberal American with a jaundiced view of social status games thinks of that.

But the "bad grammar" phenomenon is actually stranger than that, at least in English-speaking countries. In Lesson 21 I observed that speakers of English are urged not to use the preposition stranding construction, even though it's been an integral part of the language for centuries and is learned natively by virtually every native speaker of every dialect. Why on earth would *that* be stigmatized? It's not really "illogical," because a native speaker can easily say what the object of the preposition is even though it's not immediately after the preposition. The original reason for the objection, apparently, was that Latin has no such construction (or, with a bit more sophistication, that few other languages have such a construction). In other words, people who objected to preposition stranding were insisting that English grammar should be like Latin. That's perverse – English isn't Latin and isn't even descended from Latin – but it sort

---

[1] I don't know whether there is a similar phenomenon in other speech communities; if there is, a comparative study would be very interesting.

of made sense when most educated speakers of English could read (and sometimes write and even speak) Latin too. That stopped being true at least a century ago, yet the futile campaign against preposition stranding still lurches forward, zombie-like, long after any plausible rationale for it has gone over the dam.

The most baffling thing about the notion of "bad grammar" is the hold it seems to have even on highly educated speakers of English. I have heard highly qualified colleagues in the natural sciences inveigh against "bad grammar" without the slightest awareness that what they were saying was embarrassingly unscientific – no doubt because it had never occurred to them that a scientific approach to human language is feasible.

No individual can do much about this problem, but every individual can at least make sure not to be part of the problem. In principle it's simple: always remember that *all* value judgments about language are social (or political, if you like); they *never* have anything to do with language structure, nor with logic, nor with anything intrinsic to the language. Whether you want to make social judgments about the way other people talk is of course your own business, but if you do, at least get the facts right. In the twenty-first century you can expect to take some heat if you don't, and I think that's progress.

Answers to the Exercises

Lesson 2

The clauses are bracketed if there is more than one; the verbs are underlined. I have underlined not only the main verbs, but also the auxiliary verbs that go with them; as we will see in Lesson 14, English verbs are often short phrases.

1   [They didn't finish it] [because there wasn't enough time.]
2   Who caught the biggest fish?
3   Take out the garbage.
4   [If you don't know the answer,] [leave it blank.]
5   [Finally I got up over the hill,] [and I saw the most amazingly beautiful landscape.]
6   [I can't decide [whether I should take the day off.]]
7   [[How you do it] makes all the difference.]
8   [The fact [that we don't know the exact number] isn't relevant.

Lesson 3

The clauses are bracketed if there is more than one; the subjects are underlined.
1   Why did you do such a thing?
2   The man in the yellow hat finally found George in the closet.
3   [I don't think [the law should allow that.]]
4   [The weatherman said [it's going to snow tomorrow.]]
5   That statement doesn't make any sense.
6   [Please __ sit down] [and __ be quiet.] (*command, subject 'you' omitted in both clauses*)
7   John and Mary have eloped.
8   [Bert went to Chicago] [and __ found a better job.] (*clauses joined by* 'and', *subject* 'Bert' *omitted in the second clause*)

Lesson 4

This language has prefixes on its nouns, and a given noun takes a specific singular prefix and a specific plural prefix. The prefixes are paired as follows:

	(1)	(2)	(3)	(4)	(5)	(6)
Singular	m-	m-	n-	ki-	0-	u-
Plural	wa-	mi-	n-	vi-	ma-	ma- (but see below)

Class (1) includes all and only humans. Class (2) includes some names of plants, but it also includes a variety of other nouns, apparently arbitrarily. Class (3), which might have a zero prefix in both numbers (i.e. it could be an accident that all the examples begin with *n*-), also appears arbitrary. Class (4) is slightly less arbitrary, in that it includes no living creatures (although it does include at least one body part). The members of class (5) that have singulars seem to be an arbitrary list, but the members that appear only in the plural are a recognizable class: they are all collectives, used for things that can't be counted, mostly liquids. Class (6) includes abstract nouns, only one of which has a plural (because diseases can be counted); but it also includes some collectives, and these collectives are singulars rather than plurals. None are liquids; all seem to be finely divided substances.

Lesson 5

The first language does have subject-verb agreement. The agreement markers are at the beginning of the verb form, because that is the syllable that varies with the subject pronoun: 1sg. *ni*-, 2sg. *u*-, 3sg. *a*-; 1pl. *tu*-, 2pl. *m*-, 3pl. *wa*-.

The second language also has subject-verb agreement, but the system is more complicated. To judge from this paradigm,[1] the pieces are:

-*mehka*- 'find it'

ke-, any 2nd-person subject (including 'you and I')

ne-, any other 1st-person subject

-*apena*, 1pl. subject (including 'you and I')

-*apwa*, 2pl. subject

---

[1] The actual situation in this language is slightly different and even more complex, but you can only work with the information that you're given.

-*mwa*, 3sg. subject

-*mooki*, 3pl. subject

-*api*, indefinite subject ('someone')

It might be possible to break some of these pieces down still further. What is unusual about this system is the way the non-3rd-person sg. and pl. markers cross-classify so as to yield a difference between inclusive and exclusive 1pl. forms.

Lesson 6

(Direct objects, including omitted direct objects, are underlined)

1   I've never seen the Taj Mahal, and I regret it.
2   Why did they disturb the aardvark? Didn't they know __?
3   Don't elect a buffoon; the country can't survive that.
4   By the time I get to London I'll be completely exhausted.
5   I can hear the animal out there, but I can't see it.
6   I'll come get you.
7   Disregard all those irrelevant bits of information.
8   I don't have time to do that. *or* I don't have time to do that.

In example 2, the second sentence has an implied object, something like "not to do that," or "that it would be dangerous."

In example 4 there is no direct object.

In example 5, in the first clause "out there" might or might not be part of the direct object; that is, the speaker might have meant to identify the animal as "the animal out there," but (s)he might equally well have meant "I can't hear (the animal) out there," in which case the last phrase would not be part of the direct object.

The object of example 8 is not ambiguous in the same way as that of example 5, but it is unclear whether "time to do that" is a noun phrase or "to do that" indicates purpose and depends on the verb.

Lesson 7

This language marks indirect objects almost exactly like English. The preposition *kwa* seems to be the equivalent of English *to*; when it is not used to mark the indirect object, the indirect object is shifted to a position immediately following the verb.

The only new detail is that when the non-prepositional option is used with verbs other than 'give', a suffix *-er-* or *-ir-* is added immediately before the final vowel of the verb form. With the basic verb 'to give' that does not happen.

Lesson 8

In the first language, 'red' is probably a stative verb, because it appears to exhibit subject-verb agreement.

The second language does seem require number and gender agreement on its adjectives, because 'strong' (1) seems to have different endings when the subject is plural and (2) clearly has different endings when the subject is a male person, a female person, or a child.

Lesson 10

The reflexive pronouns are 2nd person because the unexpressed subject of a command is 2nd person, and the object refers to the same entity as the subject. The first sentence has a singular pronoun and the second a plural pronoun because the first command was addressed to only one person and the second to more than one.

Passive sentences:

Carthage was destroyed (by the Romans).
The smugglers are being investigated (by the FBI).
The quarkle will inevitably be blooted (by farples).

The last example shows that the syntactic system operates independently of what the words mean – even when they have no agreed meanings.

Lesson 11

The base form has a plural marker *-t*. There is a case that marks possession; there is some relationship between its markers, *-n* in the singular and *-jen* in the plural, although the details are not immediately clear. The other cases are marked by syllabic markers that are the same in sg. and pl., but in the pl. they are preceded by a plural marker *-i-*.

At least for 1st and 2nd person, possession is marked by suffixes. (We are given only the sg. markers.) If they are added to the base form, they *replace* the pl. marker, so that the possessed forms for sg. and pl. are identical. However, they are added *after* any case endings that the noun has, so at least in the cases in which the case ending follows pl. marker -*i*-, sg. and pl. possessed nouns are clearly distinguished.

Lesson 12

To judge from the nouns that refer to human beings, there is a masculine concord class and a feminine concord class; but there are also nouns that take masculine concord in the singular and feminine concord in the plural.

Lesson 13

There appears to be a case for subjects, a case for direct objects, and a case for possession, as well as five cases with specific meanings: 'with' (in the sense of doing something with a tool), 'to', 'from', 'in' or 'on', and 'together with'. The cases with the more specific meanings seem to be marked by suffixes that are attached to the object caseform, both in the singular and in the plural; that part of the case-marking system is agglutinative, although the subject, object, and possessive cases do not seem to be.

Lesson 20

Old English had negative concord; the main negative was copied onto relevant items in both directions.

Lesson 23

There was a single word that did double duty as the definite article and the demonstrative 'that'; in the latter function it contrasted with 'this'.

Glossary of Technical Terms

The number after each term is the page on which it is introduced; sometimes, when a later lesson provides much fuller discussion, two or three page numbers are given. Most of the technical terms used in Lessons 27 through 30 are not listed here, since they are discussed only in those lessons.

ablaut (70, 116): an alternation (of unknown origin) between vowels in the root syllables of grammatically related forms, such that one vowel appears in some forms and another vowel in others. Many English irregular verbs exhibit ablaut, e.g. *drive*, past *drove*, past participle *driven*; *sing, sang, sung*; *bind, bound, bound*; so do some nouns derived from them, e.g. *drift, song, bond*. In Semitic languages, such as Hebrew, ablaut is a regular part of the grammar, both in verb inflection and in derivation.

accusative (41, 91): in case-marking languages, a case used to mark the direct objects of verbs (among other things, depending on the language).

active (68): the basic or default "voice" of verbs, contrasting with **passive**.

adjective (53, 147): a major category of words that expresses qualities. Adjectives can be parts of noun phrases, modifying the noun, or complements of linking verbs; in some languages they can also be used as nouns.

adposition (48, 91): a function word that expresses the relationship of a noun phrase to the rest of the clause. See also **postposition, preposition**.

affix (79): a grammatical marker that is not an independent word, but is attached to a major word of the clause. See also **particle**.

agent (68): in a passive clause, the agent refers to the entity that would be the subject in the corresponding active clause.

agglutinative inflection (42): a system of affixes in which each affix indicates a single grammatical feature.

allegro speech (34): rapid speech that exhibits reduction or complete suppression of one or more syllables. An American English example is the pronunciation of *do you want to* that is sometimes spelled "djawanna."

ambiguous (110): having two or more clearly distinguishable meanings. See also **vague**.

antecedent (84): the noun phrase in a discourse to which a subsequent 3rd-person pronoun refers.

anterior tense (96): a verb form that indicates that the action referenced by the verb occurred before some specified point in time. The English compound tenses constructed with the auxiliary verb *have*, traditionally called "perfect" tenses, are in fact anterior tenses.

article (40, 153): a function word used to introduce noun phrases, specifying whether the noun phrase is definite or indefinite.

aspect (95): a category of verb inflection that indicates the internal structure of the action referenced by the verb (or specifically declines to indicate it).

assimilation (117): a phonological process that makes a speech sound either more similar to or identical with some other sound in the same utterance (usually, but not always, adjacent).

attributive adjective (77): an adjective inside the noun phrase headed by the noun that it qualifies. See also **predicative**.

auxiliary verb (96): a verb used together with the main verb of a clause to express grammatical information.

case (41): any of the categories in a **case-marking** system.

case-marking (41): a system of affixes that indicates the relations of noun phrases to the verb and to other words in the clause.

classifier (85): a particle that must be used when an article, demonstrative, or quantifier qualifies a noun inside a noun phrase. In a system of classifiers, the specific classifier is chosen on the basis of some semantic characteristic of the noun.

clause (13): a unit composed of a main verb, the noun phrases that stand in relation to it, and any other material that relates directly to them. A simple sentence is composed of a single clause; complex sentences are composed of multiple clauses.

comparative (173): a form of an adjective indicating a greater degree of the quality expressed by the adjective by reference to a standard of comparison, expressed or implied.

complement (52): the noun phrase or adjective introduced by a linking verb, such as *be, become,* or *seem,* that states an equivalence between subject and complement.

completive (125): a category indicating that the action of the verb has been completed; in Mandarin, marked by the particle *le.* Sometimes called perfective.

complex sentence (13): a sentence containing two or more clauses.

concord (84): a system of inflection in which each noun is assigned to a concord class and other words must have affixes marking the concord class of a noun if (a) they are within the noun phrase of which that noun is the head, or (b) they are adjective complements and the noun in question is head of the subject noun phrase, or (c) they are 3rd-person pronouns of which the noun in question is the antecedent. In some languages, such as Bantu languages, the concord class of a 3rd-person subject is also marked on the verb.

concord class (83): a class of nouns all of whose members trigger a specific concord marker, or set of markers, in a concord system.

conditional clause (99): a clause stating conditions under which the main clause is asserted to be true. Conditional clauses are usually marked by words translatable as *if* or *unless.*

conditional tense (99): a verb form stating that something would happen under stated, but unrealized, conditions. Conditional tenses are usually translatable by the English modal *would.*

conjunction (132): a particle that joins clauses or phrases. In addition to the subordinating conjunctions (see Lesson 24), English conjunctions include *and, or, but,* etc.

construct state (74): in the grammar of Semitic languages, the abbreviated form of a noun that immediately precedes the noun indicating its possessor.

continuative (122): in the grammar of Athabaskan languages, an aspect that indicates motion either through a number of scattered locations ("around") or to a destination and back.

continuous (97): an aspect that indicates that the action or state of the verb continues for a period of time. English continuous tenses are traditionally called **progressive**.

counterfactual (99): a clause that describes an action or situation under the explicit assumption that it is contrary-to-fact, i.e. not real or true.

dative (47): in case-marking languages, the case that marks the indirect object.

default (15, 27): for any grammatical parameter, the default alternative is the alternative chosen when there is no positive reason to choose any other. For verbs, the default voice is active and the default mood is indicative, and so on. Many languages have more specific defaults in their grammars; for instance, the English default noun plural marker is the one spelled *-(e)s*, while the default marker of the past tense and past participle is the one spelled *-(e)d*.

definite (40, 153): a definite noun phrase is one that the speaker expects the hearer to know about already, or to be able to infer that the referent of the noun phrase is unique; in other words, the referent of a definite noun phrase is specifically identified. (This is not a formal definition; also, there are various quirks in the ways that different languages handle definiteness.)

demonstrative (155): a grammatical word that not only indicates that a noun phrase is definite, but also locates it with reference to the speaker and/or hearer.

direct object (38): for any verb X, the noun phrase that gets Xed is the direct object.

distributive (33): a form indicating each of a set of plural entities.

dual (28): a form indicating exactly two of an entity. If a language has duals, plurals normally indicate more than two.

dummy subject (21): a pronoun with no real-world or imaginary referent, inserted merely to satisfy the requirement that a verb must have a subject.

exclusive (33): an exclusive 1st-person dual or plural does not include the person addressed; it is 1st-and-3rd persons as opposed to 1st-and-2nd.

finite verb form (115): a verb form that can be the main verb of a main clause. In languages with subject-verb agreement, finite forms exhibit such agreement; they also are usually marked for tense and/or aspect (although some nonfinite forms – i.e. infinitives and participles – can also be so marked, depending on the language).

first person (31): the speaker, and any group including the speaker.

function (25): the grammatical relations of a word or affix to other elements of a clause. For example, subject and direct object are grammatical functions.

fused inflection (42): a system of affixes in which each affix indicates two or more grammatical features together, e.g. case and number of nouns.

future tense (95): a tense that indicates that the speaker expects the action of the verb to occur or a situation to obtain at some time subsequent to the time of speaking.

gender (27): any of the concord classes of a small concord class system. Typical sets of concord classes that are commonly called genders are: masculine and feminine; masculine, feminine, and neuter; animate and inanimate. For larger concord class systems the term "gender" is usually avoided.

genitive (74): in case-marking languages, the caseform that indicates a possessor. The genitive case also commonly indicates other relationships expressed by the preposition *of* in English.

government (49): a verb or preposition is said to govern its object(s).

imperative (22): a verb mood that expresses a command.

imperfect (102, 115): in Indo-European languages, an imperfective past tense; in Semitic languages, a verb stem that expresses imperfective aspect.

imperfective (103, 115): an aspect form that indicates that the action or state expressed by the verb has an internal structure that the speaker regards as relevant.

inalienable possession (80): possession of entities that cannot be given away, such as relatives and body parts.

inclusive (33): an inclusive 1st-person dual or plural includes the person addressed; it is, in effect, 1st-and-2nd persons.

incorporation (41): the inclusion of a noun or pronoun in a verb form (as opposed to mere agreement of the verb with the noun or pronoun).

indefinite (153): an indefinite noun phrase refers to as yet unspecified member(s) of a larger class of entities.

indicative (106): the default mood of verb forms, used for making statements and asking questions that are straightforward.

indirect object (47): the noun phrase indicating the entity to which something is given or told, or for which something is done.

infinitive (115, 162): a nonfinite form of the verb used in condensed subordinate clauses. Technically an infinitive is a verbal noun, and in some languages it is also used in other ways.

inflection (5): any grammatical system according to which words assume different forms depending on their relations to other words in the clause. Many languages, such as Mandarin, have no inflection at all; others have a great deal; most fall somewhere in between.

interrogative (139): used in questions. A question is an interrogative sentence; pronouns and adverbs used to ask questions about specific details of a situation are called interrogative pronouns and adverbs.

intransitive (38): an intransitive verb is one that cannot govern a direct object.

iterative (120): a verb aspect expressing repeated action.

lexical class (27): an arbitrary inflectional class of major words. The members of different lexical classes have (at least partly) different inflectional affixes, but those affixes have exactly the same meanings and functions as those of other lexical classes.

modal verb (100): a verb that is used as an auxiliary verb and cannot be used in any other function. For instance, although *be, have,* and *do* are used as auxiliaries in English, they are also used as main verbs; that is why you also encounter forms and phrases like *being, to have*, and *had done*. By contrast, **shalling, *to shall*, and **had should* are impossible, because *shall* (past *should*) can be used only as an auxiliary; *shall* is a modal verb.[1]

momentaneous (122): in Athabaskan grammar, the default aspect; see **continuative**.

mood (105): a category of verb inflection that typically indicates the type of statement or command that a speaker is making. The default mood is the indicative, used for straightforward statements and (in most languages) questions; the imperative mood is used for commands; other moods indicate uncertainty, wishes, etc.

morpheme (197): a meaningful unit of a language, whether a word or an affix, that cannot be decomposed into smaller meaningful units.

negative concord (131): a grammatical rule by which the main negative of a sentence is copied onto grammatical words that can have a positive / negative contrast.

negative polarity item (132): a grammatical word that can be used only in negative clauses, questions, and comparative constructions. In standard English, typical negative polarity items include *any* and its compounds.

nominative (41): in case-marking languages, the case used to mark the subjects of verbs.

noun (26): a major word that refers to a real-world, abstract, or imaginary entity and can be the head of a noun phrase.

noun phrase (26): a word or phrase that can be the subject of a verb, among other functions.

null-subject language (20): a language in which the subject of a verb can be omitted even if the clause is not closely conjoined to a preceding clause.

number (26): a grammatical category indicating whether noun phrases (and things that agree with them) refer to one entity or more than one.

optative (120): a verb mood used to express the speaker's wishes.

paradigm (34): a structured list or table of all the inflectional forms of a word.

participle (168): a verbal adjective that retains some verbal syntax, such as the ability to govern objects (if the verb is transitive). In many languages participles are also used with auxiliary verbs to construct phrasal verbs.

particle (73): a grammatical marker that is an independent word.

passive (68): a clause in which the subject refers to the same entity as the direct object of the corresponding active clause.

past tense (95): a tense that indicates that the action or state expressed by the verb occurred before the time of speaking.

[1] I use this modal as an example because there are no main verbs that are homonymous with it. In addition to modal *will*, there is a main verb *to will* (past *willed*, not *would*); the two must be distinguished, as they have different meanings and different inflections. It is more obvious that modal *can* is different from *to can* in any of the latter's meanings ('to put (food) in cans', 'to fire (someone)', etc.). There are dialects of American English in which two modals can be used together, e.g. *might could* 'might be able to'; but even the combinations can be used only as auxiliaries.

past participle (68, 96): a participle that expresses past time, or time anterior to the time of the main clause. In all the languages used as examples in this book that have past participles, the past participle is passive. That is not universal; some languages have active past participles as well.

perfect (96, 108, 115): in Semitic languages, a verb stem that expresses perfective aspect. In other languages, especially Indo-European languages, the term "perfect" is used in a wide variety of ways; you should consult a standard grammar of the language in question to find out how it is used in that language.

perfective (104, 115, 120): an aspect form that indicates that the speaker does not regard the internal structure of the verb's action or state, if any, as relevant.

personal pronoun (58): a pronoun that expresses person. 1st-person pronouns refer to the speaker, or to a group containing the speaker; 2nd-person pronouns refer to the person addressed, or to a group containing the person addressed (but not usually the speaker); 3rd-person pronouns are default, referring to all other entities.

phoneme (185): a sound or group of similar sounds that constrasts with every other phoneme in a given language.

phonetics (177): the study of speech sounds as physical objects.

phonological rule (117): a rule by which one speech sound appears in place of another in a specific phonological environment (e.g. when unstressed, or when word-final, or when adjacent to some other specific speech sound).

phonology (177): the study of the organization of a language's speech sounds, including the contrasts between them that the language recognizes as significant.

plural (26): a form indicating that a noun phrase (or something agreeing with it) refers to more than one entity (or more than two, if the language has duals).

postposition (48): an adposition that follows the noun phrase that is its object.

predicative adjective (77): an adjective introduced by a linking verb. See also **attributive**.

prefix (34, 79): an affix attached before the root of a form.

preposition (48): an adposition that precedes the noun phrase that is its object.

present participle (97): a participle that expresses present time, or time simultaneous with the time of the main clause. In all the languages used as examples in this book that have present participles, the present participle is active. That is not universal; some languages have passive present participles as well.

present tense (95): a verb tense that indicates that the action or state of the verb is ongoing at the time of speaking. Many languages also use the present tense for other things, e.g. to indicate that an action will occur in the immediate future, or that something always or typically happens; some use the present tense for vividness in reporting past events.

preterite tense (102): a simple past tense, as opposed to an imperfect or an anterior tense.

progressive (97, 120): in English grammar, continuous tenses are traditionally called progressive. In Athabaskan grammar, progressive is an aspect indicating that the action of the verb is performed while moving along.

pronoun (31): a word that indicates entities identified by some grammatical characteristic; pronouns express person, or are interrogative, or indicate the noun phrase in a relative clause that refers to the head noun of the noun phrase in which the relative clause occurs, etc. Pronouns are normally entire noun phrases in themselves.

quantifier (157): a function word that indicates number or quantity, either exactly or vaguely. Numerals are quantifiers; so are such words as *some, all, many, few*, etc.

reflexive (65): a noun phrase that refers to the same entity as the subject of the clause; also, a clause with a reflexive object.

relative clause (148): a clause used as a modifier inside a noun phrase.

restrictive adjective (148): an adjective that narrows down the meaning of the noun phrase in which it occurs.

root (96): the basic part of a word that conveys its lexical meaning.

scope (137): the range of application of a negative or a general quantifier, such as *all* or *some*, within a clause.

second person (31): the person addressed, and any group including the person addressed (but not, usually, the speaker).

sentence (12): an utterance that is grammatically complete in itself.

serial verbs (126): multiple main verbs used together in a single clause.

simple sentence (13): a sentence composed of only a single clause.

singular (26): a form indicating that a noun phrase (or something agreeing with it) refers to only one entity.

stative (56): a verb or form of a verb that expresses a state.

stem (116): an incomplete inflectional form, constructed from a root, to which further inflectional affixes are attached.

stranding (146): leaving a preposition in place when its object is moved to some other position in the sentence.

subject (18): for any verb X, the noun phrase that Xes is the subject.

subject–verb agreement (20): an inflectional system in which a verb changes its form depending on the person and number of its subject (and, in some languages, other grammatical characteristics of the subject, such as concord class).

subjunctive (105): a special verb form ("mood") used to make statements that are regarded as less than certain. Many languages also use subjunctives to express a wide variety of other meanings.

subordinate clause (162): any clause of a complex sentence that is not freestanding.

subordinating conjunction (162): a conjunction that introduces a subordinate clause.

suffix (34, 79): an affix attached after the root of a form.

superlative (173): a form of an adjective indicating the greatest degree of the quality expressed by the adjective within a universe of comparison, expressed or implied.

suppletion (59): a situation in which a single paradigm is constructed from more than one root. A simple example is English *go, went, gone*, in which the past tense is made from a root completely different from that of the other forms.

syncretism (59): the expression of more than one member of a paradigm by the same form. For instance, English verbs like *sing, sang, sung* show that the past tense and past participle are different members of the paradigm, but in regular verbs like *love, loved, loved* there is syncretism between those two members.

syntax (13): the system of rules by which clauses and sentences are constructed.

tense (95): a category of verb inflection that indicates the time at which the action or state referenced by the verb takes place.

third person (31): in the category of person, any noun phrase except those denoting the speaker, the addressee, and the groups to which they belong is assigned to the third person, which is therefore the default person.

transitive (38): a transitive verb is one that can govern a direct object.

underlying forms (118): an underlying form is a (hypothetical) basic form to which phonological rules apply to yield the surface form, i.e. the form actually pronounced.

usitative (120): in Athabaskan grammar, an aspect that expresses that an action is customarily or usually done.

vague (109): having a wide range of meaning within which individual alternatives are not sharply distinguishable. See also **ambiguous**.

verb (14): the word or phrase that expresses what is going on in a clause; also, a class of words that typically fulfills that clause function.

Languages Used as Examples in the Exercises

Lesson 4: Swahili (Bantu subgroup, Niger-Congo family).
Lesson 5: Swahili; Fox (Algonkian subgroup, Algic family).
Lesson 7: Chichewa (Bantu subgroup, Niger-Congo family).
Lesson 8: Fox; Ancient Greek (Indo-European family).
Lesson 11: Finnish (Finno-Ugric subgroup, Uralic family).
Lesson 12: Tocharian B (Indo-European family).
Lesson 13: Tocharian B.

References

Aronoff, Mark. 1994. *Morphology by itself: Stems and inflectional classes.* Cambridge, MA: MIT Press.

Baker, Mark. 1988a. *Incorporation.* University of Chicago Press.

  1988b. Theta theory and the syntax of applicatives in Chichewa. *Natural Language and Linguistic Theory* 6: 353–89.

Blake, Barry J. 2001. *Case.* Cambridge University Press.

Butt, John, and Carmen Benjamin. 2011. *A new reference grammar of modern Spanish.* London: Hodder Education.

Comrie, Bernard. 1976. *Aspect.* Cambridge University Press.

Corbett, Greville G. 1991. *Gender.* Cambridge University Press.

  2000. *Number.* Cambridge University Press.

Devine, A. M., and Laurence D. Stephens. 2006. *Latin word order.* Oxford University Press.

Dresher, Bezalel Elan. 1994. The prosodic basis of the Tiberian Hebrew system of accents. *Language* 70: 1–52.

Faltz, Leonard M. 1998. *The Navajo verb: A grammar for students and scholars.* Albuquerque, NM: University of New Mexico Press.

Gelderen, Elly van. 2002. *An introduction to the grammar of English.* Amsterdam: John Benjamins.

Gesenius, Wilhelm, and Emil Kautzsch. 1910. *Gesenius' Hebrew grammar.* 2nd English edn, translated by A. E. Cowley. Oxford: Clarendon Press.

Gildersleeve, Basil L., and Gonzalez Lodge. 1895. *Latin grammar.* 3rd edn. London: Macmillan.

Ho, Yong. 2002. *Chinese–English frequency dictionary.* New York, NY: Hippocrene.

Huang, Shizhe. 2016. Adjectives. In Sybesma, Rynt, et al. (eds.), *Encyclopedia of Chinese language and linguistics* (Leiden: Brill) I.106–15.

Jackendoff, Ray. 1975. Morphological and semantic regularities in the lexicon. *Language* 51: 639–71.

Johnson, Keith. 2003. *Acoustic and auditory phonetics.* 2nd edn. Oxford: Blackwell.

Kari, James M. 1976. *Navajo verb prefix phonology.* New York, NY: Garland.

Ladefoged, Peter. 2015. *A course in phonetics.* 7th edn. Stamford, CT: Cengage Learning.

Ladefoged, Peter, and Ian Maddieson. 1996. *The sounds of the world's languages.* Oxford: Blackwell.

Pinkster, Harm. 2015. *The Oxford Latin syntax.* Vol. I. *The simple clause.* Oxford University Press.

Quirk, Randolph, et al. 1980. *A grammar of contemporary English*. 9th impression, corrected. London: Longman.

Sapir, Edward, and Harry Hoijer. 1942. *Navaho texts*. Iowa City, IA: Linguistic Society of America.

Soames, Scott, and David M. Perlmutter. 1979. *Syntactic argumentation and the structure of English*. Berkeley, CA: University of California Press.

Weir, Alison. 1991. *The six wives of Henry VIII*. New York, NY: Grove Weidenfeld.

Yip, Po-Ching, and Don Rimmington. 1997. *Chinese: An essential grammar*. London: Routledge.

Young, Robert W. 2000. *The Navajo verb system: An overview*. Albuquerque, NM: University of New Mexico Press.

Young, Robert W., and William Morgan. 1980. *The Navajo language*. Albuquerque, NM: University of New Mexico Press.